CAMPAIGN • 258

SHENANDOAH VALLEY 1862

Stonewall Jackson outmaneuvers the Union

CLAYTON & JAMES DONNELL   ILLUSTRATED BY ADAM HOOK

Series editor Marcus Cowper

First published in Great Britain in 2013 by Osprey Publishing,
Midland House, West Way, Botley, Oxford OX2 0PH, UK
43-01 21st Street, Suite 220B, Long Island City, NY 11101, USA
E-mail: info@ospreypublishing.com

© 2013 Osprey Publishing Ltd

OSPREY PUBLISHING IS PART OF THE OSPREY GROUP.

All rights reserved. Apart from any fair dealing for the purpose of private
study, research, criticism or review, as permitted under the Copyright,
Designs and Patents Act, 1988, no part of this publication may be
reproduced, stored in a retrieval system, or transmitted in any form or by
any means, electronic, electrical, chemical, mechanical, optical,
photocopying, recording or otherwise, without the prior written
permission of the copyright owner. Enquiries should be addressed to the
Publishers.

A CIP catalog record for this book is available from the British Library.

ISBN: 978 1 78096 378 5
E-book ISBN: 978 1 78096 379 2
E-pub ISBN: 978 1 78096 380 8

Editorial by Ilios Publishing Ltd, Oxford, UK (www.iliospublishing.com)
Index by Mark Swift
Typeset in Myriad Pro and Sabon
Maps by Bounford.com
3D bird's-eye view by The Black Spot
Battlescene illustrations by Adam Hook
Originated by PDQ Media, Bungay, UK
Printed in China through Worldprint Ltd.

13 14 15 16 17   10 9 8 7 6 5 4 3 2 1

AUTHORS' NOTE

We would like to thank the following people and organizations who helped
us with our research for this book. Lorraine and Jim White of The Highland
Historical Society (McDowell Battlefield); Deborah Hilty of Rose Hill Farm at
Kernstown; Jerry Casey and Gary Crawford of the Kernstown Battlefield
Association; and the Heritage Museum at Dayton, Virginia. Clayton would
like to thank his wife Donna for her continued support and Erin for her
photography and for helping to prepare the photos for publication.
Jim would like to thank his wife Amelia for her support and assistance
in the preparation of the manuscript for publication, and to his entire
family for their encouragement throughout the writing process.

ARTIST'S NOTE

Readers may care to note that the original paintings from which the
color plates in this book were prepared are available for private sale.
The Publishers retain all reproduction copyright whatsoever.
All enquiries should be addressed to:

Scorpio Gallery, 158 Mill Road, Hailsham, East Sussex, BN27 2SH, UK
scorpiopaintings@btinternet.com

The Publishers regret that they can enter into no correspondence upon this
matter.

THE WOODLAND TRUST

Osprey Publishing are supporting the Woodland Trust, the UK's leading
woodland conservation charity, by funding the dedication of trees.

Key to military symbols

XXXXX	XXXX	XXX	XX	X	III	II
Army Group	Army	Corps	Division	Brigade	Regiment	Battalion
I	•••	••	•		•	
Company/Battery	Platoon	Section	Squad	Infantry	Artillery	Cavalry
Airborne	Unit HQ	Air defense	Air Force	Air mobile	Air transportable	Amphibious
Antitank	Armor	Air aviation	Bridging	Engineer	Headquarters	Maintenance
Medical	Missile	Mountain	Navy	Nuclear, biological, chemical	Ordnance	Parachute
Reconnaissance	Signal	Supply	Transport movement	Rocket artillery	Air defense artillery	

Key to unit identification

Unit identifier — Parent unit
Commander
(+) with added elements
(-) less elements

CONTENTS

The Shenandoah Valley, February 27 to March 23, 1862

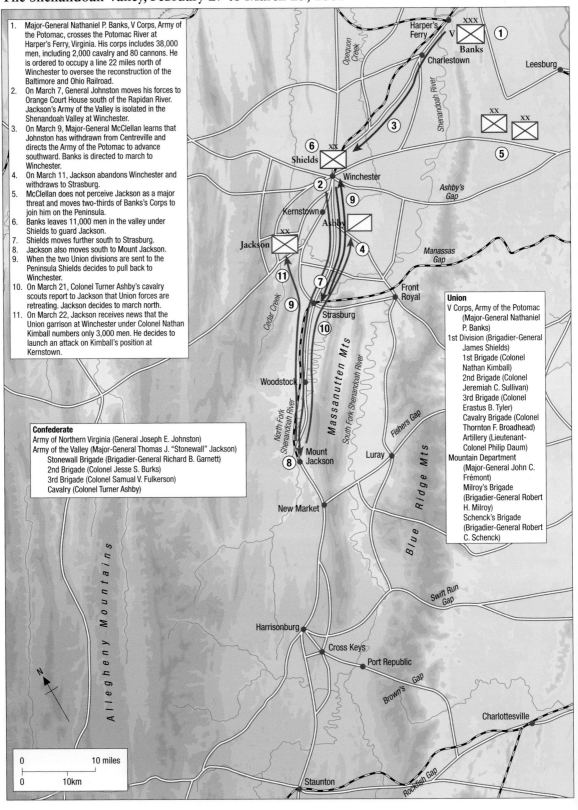

1. Major-General Nathaniel P. Banks, V Corps, Army of the Potomac, crosses the Potomac River at Harper's Ferry, Virginia. His corps includes 38,000 men, including 2,000 cavalry and 80 cannons. He is ordered to occupy a line 22 miles north of Winchester to oversee the reconstruction of the Baltimore and Ohio Railroad.
2. On March 7, General Johnston moves his forces to Orange Court House south of the Rapidan River. Jackson's Army of the Valley is isolated in the Shenandoah Valley at Winchester.
3. On March 9, Major-General McClellan learns that Johnston has withdrawn from Centreville and directs the Army of the Potomac to advance southward. Banks is directed to march to Winchester.
4. On March 11, Jackson abandons Winchester and withdraws to Strasburg.
5. McClellan does not perceive Jackson as a major threat and moves two-thirds of Banks's Corps to join him on the Peninsula.
6. Banks leaves 11,000 men in the valley under Shields to guard Jackson.
7. Shields moves further south to Strasburg.
8. Jackson also moves south to Mount Jackson.
9. When the two Union divisions are sent to the Peninsula Shields decides to pull back to Winchester.
10. On March 21, Colonel Turner Ashby's cavalry scouts report to Jackson that Union forces are retreating. Jackson decides to march north.
11. On March 22, Jackson receives news that the Union garrison at Winchester under Colonel Nathan Kimball numbers only 3,000 men. He decides to launch an attack on Kimball's position at Kernstown.

Confederate
Army of Northern Virginia (General Joseph E. Johnston)
Army of the Valley (Major-General Thomas J. "Stonewall" Jackson)
  Stonewall Brigade (Brigadier-General Richard B. Garnett)
  2nd Brigade (Colonel Jesse S. Burks)
  3rd Brigade (Colonel Samual V. Fulkerson)
  Cavalry (Colonel Turner Ashby)

Union
V Corps, Army of the Potomac (Major-General Nathaniel P. Banks)
1st Division (Brigadier-General James Shields)
  1st Brigade (Colonel Nathan Kimball)
  2nd Brigade (Colonel Jeremiah C. Sullivan)
  3rd Brigade (Colonel Erastus B. Tyler)
  Cavalry Brigade (Colonel Thornton F. Broadhead)
  Artillery (Lieutenant-Colonel Philip Daum)
Mountain Department (Major-General John C. Frémont)
  Milroy's Brigade (Brigadier-General Robert H. Milroy)
  Schenck's Brigade (Brigadier-General Robert C. Schenck)

0   10 miles
0   10km

ORIGINS OF THE CAMPAIGN

The Shenandoah Valley runs for 140 miles from rural Augusta County in western Virginia to the Potomac River at Harper's Ferry. Following a southwest to northeast course it is bounded on the west by the 5,000ft-high Allegheny Mountains, and on the east by the 4,000ft Blue Ridge Mountains. In between is a 25-mile wide ribbon of some of the best agricultural land in the state, which in the spring of 1862 was the scene of some of the fiercest fighting of the Civil War.

The Blue Ridge Mountains were a particularly formidable barrier in the 1860s. The roads were generally poor through the few isolated gaps that separated the Valley from eastern Virginia. Whoever controlled the Valley could travel virtually unseen, to suddenly emerge on an unsuspecting enemy operating in eastern Virginia. For the North, this meant being able to either seize the vital railway lines that connected the Confederate capital at Richmond with forces in Tennessee and the Mississippi Valley, or send an army cross country to attack that same capital from the west. For the South, the Valley meant protecting the grain fields and farms so vital to the food supply of the army, as well as being able to advance into Maryland and Pennsylvania and threaten the Federal capital at Washington, a concern firmly on the mind of the Federal President Abraham Lincoln.

Harper's Ferry at the northern end of the Shenandoah Valley was considered the "back door" to the heart of the Confederacy. This photo shows the confluence of the Shenandoah and Potomac rivers. (LOC)

Completed in 1809, the Long Bridge was the avenue of invasion for the Union Army into Virginia in July 1861. This photo shows the approach to Alexandria from the Washington side. (LOC)

When the war began, in April of 1861, the Shenandoah Valley also proved to be fertile recruiting ground for the newly established Provisional Army of the Confederacy. Among the organizers was a recently appointed Colonel of Virginia Volunteers, Thomas Jonathan Jackson, who only a few months before had been an instructor at the Virginia Military Institute (VMI) in Lexington, at the southern end of the Valley. Jackson's command was at Harper's Ferry where the Federal Arsenal had been the target of John Brown's abortive attempt to incite an armed slave uprising in 1859. The raid was quickly put down by a detachment of US Marines led by one Colonel Robert E. Lee.

As the Confederate Army began to take shape in the early summer of 1861, new regiments were being sent to the vicinity of Manassas Junction only 30 miles west of Washington. There, the rail line split to go west to Strasburg and the Valley, or southwest through Charlottesville to Lynchburg and points south. There also, Confederate General Pierre Gustave Toutant Beauregard, the hero of Fort Sumter, was organizing the defense of Virginia. Sixty miles further west, General Joseph Eggleston Johnston commanded the Army of the Shenandoah from Winchester, with the recently promoted Brigadier-General Jackson as his newly appointed First Brigade commander.

The Army had chosen Manassas Junction as its rallying point, both for its proximity to the Federal capital and as the most likely route for a Northern invasion. As expected, on the morning of July 16, 1861, Brigadier-General Irvin McDowell led the youthful but determined Union Army out of Washington and across the Long Bridge into Virginia. The day before, Brigadier-General Robert Patterson, who had crossed the Potomac at Williamsport on July 3, had advanced within 5 miles of Winchester. Patterson's instructions, following a pattern that would be used more than once in the spring of 1862, were to hold Johnston in the Valley while McDowell advanced on Beauregard.

On July 21 McDowell crossed Bull Run Creek and attacked the combined forces of Johnston and Beauregard in the first large-scale battle of the Civil War. The First Battle of Manassas, known to the North as First Bull Run, was a stunning victory for the South, aided in large part by the steadfastness of Brig. Gen. Jackson, who led Johnston's advance out of the Valley when Maj. Gen. Patterson pulled back to Charlestown rather than continuing to Winchester. Jackson's Brigade marched through Ashby's Gap and rode the Manassas Gap Railroad into Manassas Junction on July 19. Two days later, at the height of the battle, as the Confederate line was in danger of breaking, Confederate Brig. Gen. Barnard Bee pointed at Jackson at the top of Henry Hill and shouted, "There stands Jackson like a stone wall. Rally 'round the Virginians, boys." The Southern soldiers did rally and swept their Northern enemies from the field, and almost back to Washington, and a legend was born.

Statue of "Stonewall" Jackson on Henry Hill at the Manassas/Bull Run battlefield. Jackson commanded the First Brigade of the Army of the Shenandoah, from then on known as the "Stonewall Brigade." (Author's collection)

Before Manassas, the overwhelming opinion of those in both the North and the South was that the war would be won quickly. On April 15, the day after the surrender of Fort Sumter, President Lincoln had rather optimistically issued a proclamation calling for the enlistment of 75,000 militia for three months' service. The Confederate Congress had been somewhat more prescient, or perhaps more pessimistic, when it had issued its call on March 16 for 100,000 volunteers and militia for one year's service. On May 3, Lincoln issued a more sober call for troops, this time for 500,000 men for varying terms of service up to three years.

The euphoria the Southern people felt after the victory at Manassas had been replaced by frustration and unease as summer turned to fall and little had changed in the strategic situation. The South remained on the defensive while the North postured. On October 22 General Johnston was assigned to command the Department of Northern Virginia, headquartered at Centreville, with the Valley District, created the same day, under the command of now Major-General "Stonewall" Jackson.

The Confederate front, known as the Centreville Line, extended some 120 miles from Fredericksburg on the Rappahannock River to Jackson's headquarters at Winchester on the Opequon Creek. Jackson's force, assigned to hold the Shenandoah Valley and the Potomac River line west of Point of Rocks, Maryland, was the extreme outpost on the left. His rather tenuous line of communications ran through a small detachment at Leesburg, on the other side of the Blue Ridge, under the command of his brother-in-law Brig. Gen. Daniel Harvey Hill.

From Winchester, Jackson had access to one of the better transportation networks in the state. The Baltimore and Ohio Railroad split at Harper's Ferry, one branch going north to Martinsburg and the other south to Winchester. The Manassas Gap Railroad ran north from Mount Jackson, nearly halfway up the Valley, through Strasburg, less than twenty miles to Jackson's south, then east past Front Royal to Manassas Junction. Finally, the Virginia Central Railroad connected Staunton, near the southern end of the Valley, with Richmond.

The disposition of forces, March 1862

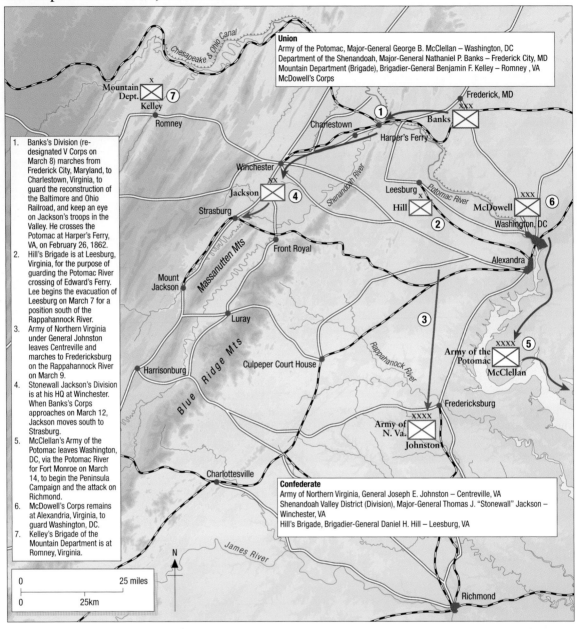

Union
Army of the Potomac, Major-General George B. McClellan – Washington, DC
Department of the Shenandoah, Major-General Nathaniel P. Banks – Frederick City, MD
Mountain Department (Brigade), Brigadier-General Benjamin F. Kelley – Romney , VA
McDowell's Corps

1. Banks's Division (re-designated V Corps on March 8) marches from Frederick City, Maryland, to Charlestown, Virginia, to guard the reconstruction of the Baltimore and Ohio Railroad, and keep an eye on Jackson's troops in the Valley. He crosses the Potomac at Harper's Ferry, VA, on February 26, 1862.
2. Hill's Brigade is at Leesburg, Virginia, for the purpose of guarding the Potomac River crossing of Edward's Ferry. Lee begins the evacuation of Leesburg on March 7 for a position south of the Rappahannock River.
3. Army of Northern Virginia under General Johnston leaves Centreville and marches to Fredericksburg on the Rappahannock River on March 9.
4. Stonewall Jackson's Division is at his HQ at Winchester. When Banks's Corps approaches on March 12, Jackson moves south to Strasburg.
5. McClellan's Army of the Potomac leaves Washington, DC, via the Potomac River for Fort Monroe on March 14, to begin the Peninsula Campaign and the attack on Richmond.
6. McDowell's Corps remains at Alexandria, Virginia, to guard Washington, DC.
7. Kelley's Brigade of the Mountain Department is at Romney, Virginia.

Confederate
Army of Northern Virginia, General Joseph E. Johnston – Centreville, VA
Shenandoah Valley District (Division), Major-General Thomas J. "Stonewall" Jackson – Winchester, VA
Hill's Brigade, Brigadier-General Daniel H. Hill – Leesburg, VA

The roads in the region would prove more critical to the maneuvering of large bodies of troops during the campaign. The Valley Turnpike ran the entire length from north to south. A New England soldier noted:

These pikes are superior as roadways to anything we have through the outlying country in the North, being graded macadamized roads from 25 to 40 feet broad, hardened with broken limestone which crushes under the weight of wheels and cements. This surface after a rain is almost as smooth, clean, and solid as a slate, and when dry a thin white coating, perhaps a quarter of an inch deep, makes dust under the constant grind of the wheels,

which rises in clouds when disturbed by travelers and settles upon their clothing making all look like millers. It grinds away shoes rapidly when a little wet, going through an army brogan in three days' marching.

Although the Valley 'Pike would figure most prominently in the campaign, there were two other macadamized roads of note. The Northwest Turnpike traversed the Allegheny Mountains and connected Winchester with Romney, and the Rockingham Turnpike connected Harrisonburg with Richmond by way of Swift Run Gap.

Jackson's Brigade rode the Manassas Gap Railroad to the battlefield at Manassas marking the first use of a railway to achieve strategic mobility. This photo shows the Railroad Bridge near Bull Run. (LOC)

Three days after Fort Sumter, Union forces burned the Federal Arsenal at Harper's Ferry. Rebel forces salvaged the machine shops and parts for 20,000 weapons vitally needed by the Confederate Army. Sketch from *Harper's Weekly*. (LOC)

Recruits poured into Washington for training at camps like Camp Cameron, named for Lincoln's first Secretary of War, near Georgetown. Regiments were sent to the front as soon as they reached full strength. (LOC)

Both sides spent the latter half of 1861 organizing, drilling and outfitting their respective armies. The South had a distinct disadvantage in manufacturing capability. The majority of its weapons had come from the various Federal arsenals in the seceding States and many of these were relatively antiquated. The North was also able to more rapidly produce and field advanced weaponry such as the Springfield Model 1861 rifled musket and the Parrott rifled cannon. Most importantly, the North had a significantly larger pool of manpower to draw on. By August 1861, the Federal Army was growing at a rate of 40,000 recruits per month. By the end of the year, when Gen. Johnston was reporting less than 60,000 men in the Department of Northern Virginia, Maj. Gen. George B. McClellan, General-in-Chief of all Union Armies, was reporting over 180,000 men available for duty in the Army of the Potomac.

The challenge for McClellan was how to best utilize his equipment and manpower advantage. His plan, as it eventually evolved, was to sail his army down the Potomac River to the Virginia Peninsula and march overland to attack Richmond. Simultaneously, McDowell with his 40,000-man corps would advance directly south from Washington to ensnare Johnston in a mighty pincer movement. McClellan's flaw was his unshakable belief that the Southern Army was decidedly larger than it actually was. Despite having over 100,000 troops under his direct command on the Peninsula, he determined that in order to successfully attack Richmond he must have the support of McDowell's corps.

Lincoln was skeptical of McClellan's arithmetic, but was willing to give him McDowell, provided a force of comparable size was left behind to protect Washington, DC. His fear was that as McClellan was maneuvering to attack Richmond the Confederate Army would sweep north and attack the Federal capital. The South could more readily surrender Richmond to a Federal Army and survive than the North could absorb the loss of its capital. At best, the sizeable contingent of Northern "Copperheads" who could accept the Confederate States of America, would cry for peace. At worst, England or some other foreign power would sense an opportunity to weaken the growing influence of the United States and supply equipment, or even troops, to the South, decidedly changing the balance of power.

Even if Johnston remained in place to defend Richmond, Jackson was still out there in the Valley. Since arriving in Winchester, the restless Stonewall, as if to defy his now famous nickname, had submitted plans for an invasion of the North; had attacked Dam No. 5 on the Chesapeake and Ohio Canal near Williamsport, Maryland; and in January, had launched an expedition to Romney, temporarily forcing the Federal garrison there to retreat north across the Potomac River. Lincoln needed Jackson contained in the Shenandoah so that he couldn't threaten Washington or move to Richmond and combine forces with Johnston. Only when that condition was met would McDowell be allowed to join McClellan.

Johnston and Confederate President Jefferson Davis were aware of the consternation within the Federal leadership, but they also knew the invasion was coming eventually, not only on the Peninsula but in the Valley as well. Major-General Nathaniel Banks was preparing to lead his 30,000-man Federal division out of Frederick City, Maryland, and march in the direction of Winchester. Johnston instructed Jackson to keep the invaders occupied in the Valley, without exposing himself to the danger of defeat, "by keeping so near the enemy as to prevent him from making any considerable detachment to reinforce McClellan, but not so near as he might be compelled to fight."

The Shenandoah Valley Campaign of 1862 proved to be a textbook study in mobility and maneuverability. Using interior lines of communication and a superior knowledge of the terrain, Jackson completely dictated the flow of events by consistently choosing the time and place to attack. In doing so, he not only upset Federal intentions in the Valley but also managed to disrupt the North's entire plan of operations for the spring of 1862. The campaign began on February 26 when Banks, with McClellan looking on, crossed the Potomac River at Harper's Ferry. As Banks advanced, Jackson withdrew as directed, but only so far as to allow him to go on the offensive at the first opportunity.

Jackson believed that destroying Dam No. 5 would dry up the Chesapeake and Ohio Canal and cut off a vital Northern supply route. This sketch shows the attack, which caused little damage and was quickly driven off. (LOC)

CHRONOLOGY

1861

July 21 — First Battle of Manassas/Bull Run (Confederate victory).

July 25 — Union Department of the Shenandoah constituted under Major-General Nathaniel P. Banks at Harper's Ferry.

July 26 — Major-General George B. McClellan assigned to command of the Union Military Division of the Potomac.

August 17 — Shenandoah Valley reassigned to the Union Department of the Potomac, headquartered at Frederick City.

October 22 — Confederate Department of Northern Virginia constituted under General Joseph E. Johnston.

Union Brigadier-General Benjamin F. Kelley occupies Romney.

November 4 — Confederate Major-General Thomas J. Jackson assumes command of the Valley District of the Department of Northern Virginia under General Joseph E. Johnston, at Winchester.

November 6 — McClellan designated General-in-Chief of all Union armies.

December 13 — Battle of Allegheny Mountain (Confederate victory).

1862

January 1–24 — Jackson's Romney Expedition.

February 26 — Major-General Banks leads Union forces across the Potomac River at Harper's Ferry towards Charlestown.

February 28 — Banks occupies Charlestown.

March 2 — Banks occupies Martinsburg.

March 8 — Presidential War Order No. 2 reorganizes the Federal Army of the Potomac. Banks assigned to command of V Corps.

March 9 — General J. E. Johnston withdraws from Centreville to Culpeper Courthouse.

March 11 — Presidential War Order No. 3 relieves McClellan as General-in-Chief, retains him as commander of the Army of the Potomac.

Union Department of Western Virginia redesignated as the Mountain Department.

March 12 — Banks occupies Winchester.

Jackson withdraws to Mount Jackson.

March 17 — Banks directed to leave Major-General James Shields's division at Strasburg and withdraw to Manassas Junction.

March 19–20	Shields temporarily occupies Strasburg before withdrawing to Winchester.	May 23	Battle of Front Royal (Confederate victory).
March 22	Skirmish at Kernstown.	May 24	Skirmish at Middletown.
March 23	Battle of Kernstown (Union victory).		Banks withdraws from Strasburg.
March 25	Banks occupies Strasburg.	May 25	First Battle of Winchester (Confederate victory).
	Jackson withdraws to Mount Jackson.		Banks withdraws from Winchester to Williamsport.
March 29	Major-General John C. Frémont assumes command of the Mountain Department at Wheeling.		Brigadier-General Rufus Saxton assumes command of Union troops in vicinity of Harper's Ferry.
April 1	Banks occupies Woodstock.		
April 2	Jackson withdraws to Rude's Hill.	May 30	Major-General James Shields occupies Front Royal.
April 4	Union Department of the Rappahannock constituted under Major-General Irvin McDowell.	May 31	Jackson withdraws to Strasburg.
		June 2	Shields arrives at Luray.
	Union Department of the Shenandoah redesignated as an Independent Command under Major-General Banks.	June 5	Banks marches to Winchester.
		June 6	Jackson and Ewell arrive in vicinity of Port Republic.
April 19	Banks occupies New Market.		
	Jackson withdraws to Elk Run Valley.		Frémont arrives at Harrisonburg.
April 25	Banks occupies Harrisonburg.		Skirmish at Cedar Ridge.
April 27	Union Brigadier-General Robert Milroy occupies McDowell.	June 8	Battle of Cross Keys (Confederate victory).
April 30	Jackson marches to Staunton.	June 9	Battle of Front Royal (Confederate victory).
	Ewell marches to Elk Run Valley.		Frémont withdraws to Harrisonburg.
May 8	Battle of McDowell (Confederate victory).		Shields withdraws to Luray.
May 9	Milroy withdraws to Franklin.		Jackson moves to Weyer's Cave.
May 13	Banks withdraws to Strasburg.	June 17	Jackson marches to the Peninsula.
May 17	Jackson arrives in Harrisonburg.	June 26	Union Department of the Rappahannock, Department of the Shenandoah, and Mountain Department consolidated under the Army of Virginia.
May 20	Jackson arrives in New Market.		
	Ewell arrives in Luray.		

OPPOSING COMMANDERS

Abraham Lincoln took his role as Commander-in-Chief very seriously and spent considerable time and effort finding generals who would fight. (LOC)

In the summer of 1861, both the North and South were attempting to come to grips with the fact that one battle was not going to end the war, as so many had believed before Manassas/Bull Run. When the Confederate commanders called off their pursuit of the retreating Federal Army, which enabled the Union soldiers to return to their camps around Washington, the real work of war began. Federal President Abraham Lincoln and Confederate President Jefferson Davis fully exercised their roles as Commanders-in-Chief as specified in their respective Constitutions. Lincoln relied on the wisdom and experience of Major-General Winfield Scott, veteran of the War of 1812 and hero of the Mexican War, as his General-in-Chief. When Scott retired in November, Maj. Gen. McClellan temporarily assumed that role. Jefferson Davis relied on Gen. Robert E. Lee, who had been offered and refused command of the Union Army by Scott in April 1861. At the time of the Shenandoah Valley Campaign, President Lincoln was pushing his field commanders to go on the offensive, while President Davis was resolved to fight a defensive campaign as he struggled with the realization that the resources of the South could never match those of the North. McClellan saw the Federal forces deployed in the Valley as a source of manpower for his own Peninsula Campaign. Jackson saw the Valley both as a gateway to the North, to attack the industrial strength of the North head-on, and as a means of tying up Federal manpower to take pressure off of the main Southern Army around Richmond. "If this Valley is lost, Virginia is lost," Jackson stated at the outset of the campaign.

CONFEDERATE COMMANDERS

Major-General Thomas Jonathan "Stonewall" Jackson graduated 18th in a class of 70 from West Point in 1846. He served as lieutenant of artillery under Winfield Scott in Mexico and was brevetted captain and major for bravery. After the Mexican War he became a professor of artillery tactics and natural philosophy at the Virginia Military Institute in Lexington, Virginia. As the senior Confederate commander in the Valley he constantly looked for opportunities to attack and defeat his Federal adversaries.

General Joseph Eggleston Johnston graduated 13th in a class of 46 from West Point in 1829. He served nearly his entire career in the army, rising steadily through the ranks. He was cited for bravery in both the Florida Indian wars and the Mexican War. On April 22, 1861, when he resigned his commission following the secession of his native Virginia, he was serving as Quartermaster-General, one of only four general officers in the US Army. At the time of Jackson's Valley Campaign, Johnston was commander of the Department of Northern Virginia, trying desperately to determine the best way to defend Richmond against the impending Federal attack. He looked to Jackson to keep the Northern leadership distracted with events in the Valley.

Major-General Richard Stoddert Ewell graduated 13th in a class of 42 from West Point in 1840 and served with the 1st US Dragoons until April, 1861. Like Jackson and Johnston, he served in the Mexican War. Initially appointed as a lieutenant-colonel in the Confederate cavalry, he quickly rose to the rank of brigadier-general and led a brigade at Manassas. In January 1862 he was promoted to major-general, and "Ewell's Division" played a key role in the Valley Campaign, although he initially had serious doubts about Jackson's sanity.

Jefferson Davis had been Franklin Pierce's Secretary of War. During that time, he increased the size of the regular army and directed the adoption of the .58-cal. rifled musket as the standard army firearm. (LOC)

Jackson achieved international renown following the Valley campaign. This photo shows him as a lieutenant-general and Lee's "right arm" before his untimely death at Chancellorsville in 1863. (LOC)

Major-General Edward "Allegheny" Johnson also graduated from West Point and served in the Seminole Wars and Mexican War. After the outbreak of the Civil War he took command of the 12th Georgia Infantry, a unit that would achieve considerable recognition for its performance at the battle of McDowell. Fighting near Camp Allegheny in western Virginia in December 1861, he successfully fought off an attack led by Union Brigadier-General Robert H. Milroy, earning for himself his distinctive nickname. He would face Milroy again while fighting with Jackson at the battle of McDowell, where he was severely wounded.

Brigadier-General Turner Ashby was the son of a veteran of the War of 1812 and grandson of a veteran of the American Revolution. He served as a Captain of Volunteers in the Virginia Militia during the 1850s, and joined the Confederate army when the war began. He was appointed commander of the 7th Virginia Cavalry, and spent considerable time harassing Federal troops in the Northern Valley until Jackson's arrival at Winchester in November 1861. In March 1862, it was his report to Jackson that led to the battle of Kernstown. In June 1862 at Chestnut Ridge, near Harrisonburg, he was fatally shot while attempting to ambush Federal troops pursuing Jackson just prior to the battle of Cross Keys.

UNION COMMANDERS

Major-General Nathaniel Prentiss Banks was born in Massachusetts and served as a US Congressman and Governor of the state until 1861. At the outbreak of the war, he offered his services to President Lincoln, who appointed him a Major-General of Volunteers in return for his support for the war effort in his home state. He was assigned to command the Department of the Shenandoah, which became the V Corps of the Army of the Potomac in March 1862. During the campaign, he was constantly being pulled back and forth between Lincoln and McClellan.

Major-General John Charles Frémont earned the nickname "Pathfinder" for his journeys across the Rocky Mountains prior to the war. He entered politics in California, and in 1856 became the first Republican candidate for the Presidency, losing to James Buchanan. He was appointed a Major-General of Volunteers in July 1861 and sent to command the Western Department in St. Louis, Missouri. He served as commander of the Mountain Department during the Valley Campaign, running afoul of President Lincoln for his continued foot-dragging when he was ordered to go after Jackson.

Major-General George Brinton McClellan graduated second in the West Point class of 1846 and served with distinction in the Mexican War, winning brevet to captain. When the Civil War began, he was appointed a Major-General of the Militia Volunteers of Ohio, and subsequently became the commander of the Department of Ohio for the Federal Army. He won distinction at the battles of Philippi and Rich Mountain in June and July 1861, and was called to Washington, DC, to take command of the Army of the Potomac on July 26, 1861. He became General-in-Chief of all Union forces in November. McClellan transformed the Union Army into a formidable fighting force at a time when 40,000 recruits per month were entering Federal military service. At the time of the Valley Campaign he was in a running feud with President Lincoln over the number of troops he believed he needed to fight his Peninsula Campaign in southeast Virginia.

Brigadier-General Nathan Kimball served as a captain in the 2nd Indiana Volunteers during the Mexican War. He became colonel of the 14th Indiana Infantry in 1861, and fought at the battle of Cheat Mountain in September of that year, defeating forces under Robert E. Lee. He was subsequently appointed commander of the First Brigade in Brigadier-General James Shields's division of Banks's corps. At the battle of Kernstown he acted as the commander on the field after Shields was wounded, and defeated Stonewall Jackson in the only battle that he lost during the campaign. As such, he was the only Union commander to defeat both Lee and Jackson on the field of battle.

Brigadier-General Robert Huston Milroy graduated from Captain Partridge's Academy in Norwich, Vermont, in 1843 with a Master of Military Sciences Degree and served as a captain in the 1st Indiana Volunteers during the Mexican War.

At the outbreak of the Civil War he became colonel of the 9th Indiana Infantry, serving in Western Virginia. He was promoted to brigadier-general and commanded the Cheat Mountain District of Frémont's Mountain Department during the Valley Campaign. He fought forces under Jackson and Johnson at the battle of McDowell on May 8, 1862, surprising the Confederate generals by initiating the battle when they expected him to stay on the defensive.

Banks was rewarded for his support to President Lincoln with an appointment as Major-General of Volunteers, one of many "political generals" on the Union side. Banks served in a number of positions during the war. (LOC)

A significant difference between the Union and Confederate commanders in the Valley campaign was that Jackson was almost always on or near the field of battle, while Banks, and later Frémont, always seemed to be somewhere else. At Kernstown, Banks was on his way to Harper's Ferry, expecting to return to Manassas. At McDowell, he remained at Harrisonburg, never even aware that the battle was being fought. At Front Royal, he was 15 miles away at Strasburg, worrying about Jackson attacking him from the south, while being completely unaware that Jackson and Ewell, with a force several times larger than his own, were on his flank. During the battles of Cross Keys and Port Republic, he never got closer than Winchester, while first Frémont, then Brig. Gen. Erastus B. Tyler took on Jackson and Ewell. Frémont was criticized by Milroy for being far behind the lines at Cross Keys, and was surprised to find that Jackson and Ewell had gotten away the next day, but that didn't stop him from taking credit for defeating them in both battles.

OPPOSING FORCES

Winfield "Old Fuss and Feathers" Scott led the assault on Mexico City during the Mexican War. Many future Civil War generals served under Scott in Mexico. (LOC)

Lee was offered the command of the Union Army by Scott in April 1861, but refused to take up arms against his native Virginia. This photo shows Lee as a lieutenant-general. (LOC)

THE UNION ARMY

The 8,500 troops that Nathaniel Banks led over the Potomac River on February 26, 1862, to open the Shenandoah Valley campaign, were mostly green volunteers, with a smattering of veterans from the Mexican War. The 84th Pennsylvania Infantry Volunteers were just four days removed from training camp when they joined Banks's division on January 2. They were accompanied by the similarly untested 110th Pennsylvania from Harrisburg. The 29th and 67th Ohio had spent their war service guarding prisoners at Camp Chase, a military staging, training, and prison camp in Columbus, Ohio. The more experienced men came from the "western" units, like the 1st (West) Virginia, 7th Ohio, and 14th Indiana regiments which had seen some action in the West Virginia Campaign in the summer and fall of 1861. Of that group, the soldiers of the 4th Ohio had been in continuous field service for six months by January 1862.

Banks, himself, was a political appointee, achieving his position due to his strong support for President Lincoln, and a common conception that the Massachusetts units raised under Banks's governorship, were well trained and well equipped. Banks's first military command was at Annapolis, Maryland, where he was directed to enforce support for the Union in a slave-holding state that threatened to secede. When Brigadier-General Robert Patterson allowed Confederate General Johnston's men to escape the Valley and save the battle of First Manassas for the Confederacy, Banks was sent to take his place in the upper Potomac region.

Banks's lieutenants were, like the troops they led, a mix of experienced and raw commanders. Commanding Banks' First Division was Alpheus Williams, a lawyer by trade, who had served as a lieutenant-colonel of the 1st Michigan Infantry during the Mexican War, but had seen no action. Brigadier-General James Shields, commander of Banks's Second Division, had fought with distinction under Winfield Scott, the recently retired General-in-Chief of the Union Army, in that same conflict, being twice wounded, before returning to civilian life. Brigadier-General Nathan Kimball, commander of Shields's First Brigade, another Mexican War veteran, raised a company of volunteers for the 2nd Indiana Infantry and received distinction at the battle of Buena Vista. Others, like Brigadier-General Erastus Tyler, Shields's Third Brigade commander, had no formal military training before the war.

Over 90,000 men responded to Lincoln's initial call for 90-day volunteers. A more realistic call for 500,000 for three years was made on May 3, 1861. This sketch from *Frank Leslie's Illustrated Newspaper* shows a New York recruiting station. (LOC)

This was an army of volunteers, raised, outfitted, and trained by the individual states. One fourth was immigrants, with Germans, Irish, Canadians, and British being the most common. This led to unit distinction. The 55th New York Infantry was the Gardes Lafayette. The 39th New York Infantry was the Garibaldi Guard. The 58th New York Infantry was the Polish Legion. Additionally, every Southern state had men in the Union Army.

The reasons for their volunteering varied widely. In the beginning there was little sympathy for the emancipation cause, but as the war progressed and they came more into contact with the evidence of slavery, many became abolitionists. Many felt it was more honorable to volunteer than wait to be drafted, once the Federal government passed conscription laws. Army pay proved to be a powerful motivator. The North had taken in two million immigrants in the 1850s, and many were subjected to poverty and

More than 40,000 recruits per month arrived in Washington in 1861. The total number of troops who served in the Union Army during the war was more than 2.4 million, compared to about 1 million Confederates. This sketch shows Lincoln and Scott reviewing the troops. (LOC)

unemployment. The $13 a month a Union soldier received was good pay for the time, and many were able to send money home on a consistent basis. One theme, however, transcended all others: the belief in the Union and the need for the country to remain whole. That was worth fighting for. The Valley itself had many pro-Union citizens, although a number had been rounded up and imprisoned. When Banks marched into Winchester on March 12, the Stars and Stripes appeared in more than one house to greet the invading host.

THE CONFEDERATE ARMY

"Jackson's Division" started out with about 5,000 men including three infantry brigades with 12 regiments, plus Ashby's 7th Virginia Cavalry supported by Chew's Virginia Battery. It included such veteran units as the "Stonewall Brigade," so named because it was Jackson's original command at the battle of First Manassas. During the Valley Campaign, "Virginia's First Brigade" was commanded by Brigadier-General Richard Garnett, then by Brigadier-General Charles Winder when Garnett was relieved of duty by Jackson after First Kernstown. All of the division's regiments were Virginia volunteers. The companies of the Stonewall Brigade came predominantly from the western part of Virginia. These were Valley men fighting on Valley soil.

While most were farmers or farm laborers, the third most common were students from the Virginia Military Institute, Washington College, and the University of Virginia. Second Brigade companies were recruited in Central and Southwest Virginia. The men from the First Virginia Battalion, also called the "Irish Battalion," were Irish laborers from the major cities of Virginia. Third Brigade companies came from Richmond and Central and Southern Virginia counties. Allegheny Johnson's men came from the Shenandoah Valley and Central and West Central Virginia counties.

Jackson's forces expanded significantly during the campaign, reaching an eventual peak of 17,000 men with the addition of Ewell's troops in late May. Still, it remained greatly outnumbered by the various Union armies opposing it, those totaling 52,000 men by June 1862.

Despite the discrepancy in numbers, Jackson's men didn't have to look far for motivation to stand and fight. They had been invaded by the soldiers of a government that not only threatened their land and their homes, but who also threatened to forever change their way of life. And there was a prevalent belief throughout the South that a southern man was worth ten of anyone from the North. There was no shortage of courage in the Confederacy. Where Jackson's men came up short was in arms and armament.

INFANTRY

Since the States were so much a part of the recruitment of regiments, the appointment of officers was heavily political. Governors often selected Colonels based on their ability to raise regiments, rather than on any military ability. Lieutenants were elected by the enlisted men, often because they had been heavily involved in their recruitment.

Jackson began 1862 with some 7,500 volunteers, 664 cavalrymen, and 2,300 militiamen. To call the militia militarily competent was a gross over-exaggeration. Their primary activities in the pre-war days included parades and ceremonial functions. They had an aversion to military discipline and training, and integrated poorly with Jackson's volunteers. Jackson had discovered more than once during the Romney campaign that they were virtually incapable of independent operations, and he quickly relegated them to guarding passes through the mountains, a task they were no more successful at. The situation took care of itself when Governor Letcher ordered all Virginia militiamen drafted into existing volunteer units on March 29.

Both sides lost men to battle. Numbers vary, but by the best estimates, the North suffered approximately 4,625 casualties (killed, wounded, or missing) in the six major battles of the campaign, while the South lost 2,800. About 20 percent of those were killed or mortally wounded. Many died after the battle due to the rudimentary capabilities of the Medical services, or from the most prevalent killer – disease. Estimates are that four times as many soldiers died from disease as were killed in action.

Infantry weapons on both sides varied widely. Although some units entered service with smooth bore flintlock muskets, the standard-issue firearm in the regular army in 1861, was the Model 1855 Springfield rifled musket. Unfortunately, production was geared towards supporting a standing army of less than 20,000 officers and men, not the hundreds of thousands that were starting to come into service. There were approximately 150,000 shoulder arms fit for use throughout the Confederacy in 1861, of which about 20,000 were rifled. Both governments turned to Europe for arms. In February 1862 Banks reported three regiments with Austrian rifled muskets, one with Belgian, one with British Enfields, and two with Springfield altered smooth bores. The Federal government was particularly successful at shutting off the flow of arms to the Confederacy, particularly due to the Union naval blockade of Southern ports. Many of Jackson's men brought their own guns when they enlisted, but these were often inferior .54-cal. Mexican War era weapons, and some of the militia units had Revolutionary War era muskets. The seizure of the Federal Arsenal at Harper's Ferry the previous year gave the Confederacy the equipment it needed to manufacture rifles and rifled muskets, but production was still woefully inadequate in the spring of 1862.

Smoothbore cannons were the primary field pieces for both sides in 1861. (LOC)

ARTILLERY

Artillery was a supporting branch to the Infantry. Union batteries generally had six guns, while Confederate batteries had four, although these numbers fluctuated throughout the war. Organizationally, Banks's forces maintained artillery brigades, composed of five batteries, with each battery assigned the same caliber gun. Confederate battalions of four batteries, often of mixed caliber weapons, were assigned directly to the infantry division, which meant they were often more dispersed across the battlefield.

Jackson initially had at his disposal the Rockbridge and West Augusta Batteries in the Stonewall Brigade, and Pleasant's and Danville in the Second and Third Brigades. The artillery units increased with the arrival of Ewell's Division. Jackson's artillery units were named either for the places they originated, such as Rockbridge or Danville, or after their commanders; for example, Carpenter's, Pleasant's, and Chew's Batteries. The latter was a horse artillery battery that served with Ashby's 7th Virginia Cavalry. Horse artillery was light, fast-moving, and fast-firing. It consisted of light cannons or howitzers pulled by two-wheeled carriages. These units were the precursor to self-propelled artillery. Jackson certainly knew the value of artillery on the battlefield. During the Mexican War, he had decisively commanded the artillery during the battle of Chapultepec. At First Manassas, it was his unit that attacked and overwhelmed the batteries of Griffin and Ricketts on Henry Hill at the critical moment of the battle.

Field artillery was employed primarily as an anti-personnel weapon. Artillerymen loaded different types of ammunition, such as shot, shell, grapeshot, and canister, depending on the action on the field at any one time. Howitzers, most commonly of 12-pdr and 24-pdr variations, usually accompanied the cannons. Howitzers fired explosive shells in a higher trajectory over shorter ranges than cannons, and were optimized for use against troops massed behind fortifications or other types of protected positions.

Rifled guns gave Banks a significant advantage. Rifled barrels had spiral grooves etched into the inside surface of the barrel that spun a conical shell, increasing range and accuracy. The most common was the Parrott rifle, invented by Robert Parrott in 1860. Parrott guns came in many sizes from 10-pdr, like those used by Captain Clark's Battery E, 4th US Artillery at the battle of Kernstown, all the way up to 300-pounders (not used in the campaign). The effective range of a ten-pound Parrott exceeded 1800 yards. The preponderance of rifled guns in the Union army significantly determined the progress of the battles of Kernstown and Port Republic, and almost changed the outcome of the battle of Front Royal.

The most common field artillery piece in 1861 was the 12-pdr smoothbore model of 1857 known as the "Napoleon." It could fire solid shot projectiles up to 1,600 yards. (LOC)

CAVALRY

If Banks had an advantage in artillery, Jackson used his cavalry much more effectively. Its primary purpose was reconnaissance, but it was also used to screen the movements of the infantry, and harass enemy forces. Ashby's men came primarily from the counties of the Upper Shenandoah counties as well as Fauquier and Loudoun counties. They knew their way around the valley. The Confederate cavalry spent considerable time conducting raids on railroads and lines of communications, while the Union cavalry was focused on protecting those same entities.

On the battlefield cavalry would often be called upon to charge the enemy's guns, which are posted on a hill in this sketch. The enemy's line has met the charge, and is trying to save the guns, which are hurrying to the rear "on mount." (LOC)

Even though the Union entered the war with five Regular Army cavalry regiments, 101 of the 176 experienced officers resigned to join the Confederacy. That, combined with the fact that a higher percentage of its citizenry was accustomed to being on horseback in the rural South, compared to those from the industrialized North, gave the Confederate cavalry a decided edge early in the war. During the Valley campaign, Jackson had a superior cavalry commander, Turner Ashby, and superior horsemen. Banks had a collection of men with horses.

Ashby had been a reluctant farmer when the war broke out, but was an excellent horseman and had been responsible for organizing a mounted company to protect the locals from the road crews brought in to build the Manassas Gap Railroad across the Blue Ridge in 1855. Ashby and his men formed the core of the 7th Virginia Cavalry. Ashby's troops were armed largely with what they brought from home, were poorly uniformed, and furnished their own mounts.

Ashby received permission from the War Dept. to organize a mounted cavalry unit under the command of one of Jackson's former artillery students, Robert Preston Chew. Chew's Battery consisted of a long-range Blakely gun, a medium-range, 3in. rifled piece, and a stubby, short-range 12-pdr howitzer.

Civil War battles were usually fought by troops in formation. The most common deployment was the regimental "line-of-battle" two ranks deep, as in this sketch of the battle of Savage's Station during the Peninsula Campaign. (LOC)

During the campaign, the most significant use of cavalry to influence the outcome of a battle occurred when Confederate Colonel Thomas Flournoy's 6th Virginia Cavalry forced the surrender of the Union garrison at Front Royal. The most significant cavalry failure was caused by the inability of Jackson's cavalry commanders to chase down Banks's fleeing army following the battle of Winchester.

TACTICS

During the campaign, the North was more concerned about maintaining a presence in the Valley, than in actually fighting any battles. This was just as well for Jackson who believed in speed and maneuverability, always endeavoring to bring his strength against the enemy's weakness. Military officers are students of history, and Jackson was no exception. It was said that he carried three books in his saddlebags at all time: a Bible, a dictionary, and the Military Maxims of Napoleon. "My idea is that the best mode of fighting is to reserve your fire till the enemy get – or you get them – to close quarters. Then deliver one deadly, deliberate fire- and charge!" (Jackson).

In March 1862 Jackson discovered Jedediah Hotchkiss. Hotchkiss had been a member of the Augusta Militia, and volunteered for service as an engineer on Jackson's staff. He made maps for Garnett and General Lee's campaign in the mountains in the fall of 1861. Jackson asked Hotchkiss to make him a map of the valley from Harper's Ferry to Lexington, showing all of the major strategic places. His maps were accurate and detailed and certainly provided Jackson more aid in the movement of his troops and the ability to mount surprise attacks on Union forces than all the other militiamen in the Valley.

Banks had his own Hotchkiss. His name was David Hunter Strother, and he served as Assistant Topographical Engineer on Banks's staff, as well as a very successful intelligence officer. Strother was born in Martinsburg, Virginia, and was a writer for *Harper's Monthly Magazine*. His articles included details not only of the Valley, but of the whole South, and gained him a nationwide reputation. His support for the Union led him to be loathed by Southerners. Among his many talents was the creation of a spy network that kept Banks and his staff well informed of enemy movements throughout the campaign.

When Banks advanced to open the campaign in February 1862, Jackson was forced to withdraw south, up the Valley. This induced the Northern leadership to believe that he was incapable of mounting a threat, and they began to strip away Banks' forces and redeploy them eastward to join the build-up for McClellan's Peninsula campaign. By the end of March, Jackson was convinced that Banks was about to abandon the Valley altogether, and the vastly reduced Union Corps was vulnerable to attack.

ORDERS OF BATTLE

CONFEDERATE ARMY

VALLEY DISTRICT, DEPARTMENT OF NORTHERN VIRGINIA   Maj. Gen. Thomas J. Jackson

JACKSON'S DIVISION	Maj. Gen. Thomas J. Jackson
First Brigade "The Stonewall Brigade"	Brig. Gen. Richard B. Garnett (battle of Kernstown), Brig. Gen. Charles S. Winder
2nd Virginia Infantry	Col. J. W. Allen
4th Virginia Infantry	Lt. Col. Charles A. Ronald
5th Virginia Infantry	Col. William H. Harman
27th Virginia Infantry	Col. John Echols
33rd Virginia Infantry	Col. Arthur C. Cummings
Rockbridge Battery, Virginia Artillery	Capt. James H. Wateres
West Augusta Battery, Virginia Artillery	
Carpenter's Battery	Capt. Joseph Carpenter
Second Brigade	Col. Jesse S. Burks (Kernstown), Col. John A. Campbell
21st Virginia Infantry	Lt. Col. John M. Patton, Jr.
42nd Virginia Infantry	Lt. Col. D. A. Langhorne
48th Virginia Infantry	Col. John A. Campbell
1st Virginia Infantry Battalion (The Irish Battalion)	Capt. D. B. Bridgford
Pleasants' Virginia Battery	Lt. James Pleasants
Third Brigade	Col. Samuel V. Fulkerson (Kernstown), Brig. Gen. William B. Taliaferro
23rd Virginia Infantry	Lt. Col. Alexander G. Taliaferro
37th Virginia Infantry	Lt. Col. R. P. Carson
Danville Battery, Virginia Artillery	Lt. A. C. Lanier
Cavalry	
7th Virginia Cavalry	Col. Turner Ashby
Chew's Virginia Battery	Capt. R. P. Chew

Jackson's Division participated in each of the six battles of the campaign. At McDowell, the First Brigade supported Allegheny Johnson's Brigade (Army of the Northwest), while the cavalry and artillery did not participate in the actual fighting. Following Ashby's death on June 6, Colonel Thomas Munford became Jackson's Cavalry Commander. At Cross Keys, only the Second Brigade supported Ewell's Division.

ARMY OF THE NORTHWEST	Brig. Gen. Edward Johnson
Johnson's Brigade	Brig. Gen. Edward Johnson
12th Georgia Infantry	Col. Z. T. Conner
25th Virginia Infantry	Col. George H. Smith
31st Virginia Infantry	Lt. Col. W. L. Jackson
44th Virginia Infantry	Col. W. C. Scott
52nd Virginia Infantry	Col. Michael G. Harman
58th Virginia Infantry	Col. Samuel H. Letcher

The Army of the Northwest participated only in the battle of McDowell. Brigadier-General Johnson was wounded during the battle and was carried from the field. Jackson subsequently divided Johnson's command between his own and Ewell's Division.

EWELL'S DIVISION	Maj. Gen. Richard S. Ewell
Second Brigade	Col. W. C. Scott
1st Maryland Infantry	Col. Bradley T. Johnson
44th Virginia Infantry	Col. W. C. Scott
52nd Virginia Infantry	Lt. Col. James H. Skinner
58th Virginia Infantry	Col. Samuel H. Letcher
Fourth Brigade	Brig. Gen. Arnold Elzey
12th Georgia Infantry	Col. Zephaniah T. Conner
13th Virginia Infantry	Col. James A. Walker
25th Virginia Infantry	Lt. Col. Patrick Duffy
31st Virginia Infantry	Col. John S. Hoffman
Seventh Brigade	Brig. Gen. Isaac Trimble
15th Alabama Infantry	Col. James Cantey
21st Georgia Infantry	Col. John T. Mercer
16th Mississippi Infantry	Col. Carnot Posey
21st North Carolina Infantry	Col. William W. Kirkland
Eighth Brigade	Brig. Gen. Richard Taylor
6th Louisiana Infantry	Col. Isaac G. Seymour
7th Louisiana Infantry	Col. Harry T. Hays
8th Louisiana Infantry	Col. Henry B. Kelly
9th Louisiana Infantry	Col. Leroy A. Stafford
Wheat's Battalion (Louisiana Tigers)	Maj. Chatham Roberdeau Wheat
Artillery	Col. Stapleton Crutchfield
Brockenbrough's Battery	Capt. John B. Brockenbrough
Courtney's Battery	Capt. A. R. Courtney
Lusk's Battery	Capt. John A. M. Lusk
Raine's Battery	Capt. Charles I. Raine
Rice's Battery	Capt. William H. Rice
Cavalry Brigade	Col. Thomas T. Munford, Brig. Gen. George H. Steuart (Winchester only)
2nd Virginia Cavalry	Col. Thomas T. Munford
6th Virginia Cavalry	Col. Thomas Flournoy
Chew's Battery	Capt. R. Preston Chew

Ewell's Division participated in the battles of Front Royal, Winchester, Cross Keys, and Port Republic.

UNION ARMY

V CORPS, ARMY OF THE POTOMAC
Maj. Gen. Nathaniel P. Banks

SHIELDS'S DIVISION	Brig. Gen. James Shields
First Brigade	Col. Nathan Kimball
14th Indiana Infantry	Lt. Col. William Harrow
8th Ohio Infantry	Col. Samuel S. Carroll
67th Ohio Infantry	Lt. Col. Alvin C. Voris
84th Pennsylvania Infantry	Col. William G. Murray
Second Brigade	Col. Jeremiah C. Sullivan
5th Ohio Infantry	Lt. Col. John H. Patrick
39th Illinois Infantry	Col. Thomas O. Osborn
13th Illinois Infantry	Lt. Col. Robert S. Foster
62nd Ohio Infantry	Col. Francis B. Pond
Third Brigade	Col. Erastus B. Tyler
7th Indiana Infantry	Lt. Col. John F. Creek
7th Ohio Infantry	Lt. Col. William R. Creighton
29th Ohio Infantry	Lt. Col. Lewis P. Buckley
110th Pennsylvania Infantry	Col. William D. Lewis, Jr.
1st West Virginia Infantry	Col. Thomas Thoburn
Cavalry Brigade	Col. Thornton F. Brodhead
1st Michigan Cavalry (Battalion)	Lt. Col. Joseph T. Copeland
1st Ohio Cavalry	Capt. Nathan D. Menken
1st Squadron	Capt. John Keys
Pennsylvania Cavalry	Maj. B. F. Chamberlain
1st West Virginia Battalion	
Independent Companies,	Capt. Henry A. Cole,
Maryland Cavalry	Capt. William Firey,
	Capt. John Horner
Artillery	Lt. Col. Philip Daum
Battery H, 1st Ohio Artillery	Capt. James F. Huntington
Battery L, 1st Ohio Artillery	Capt. Lucius N. Robinson
Battery E, 4th US Artillery	Capt. Joseph C. Clark, Jr.
Battery B, West Virginia Artillery	

Shields's Division participated in the battles of Kernstown, Cross Keys, and Port Republic. Shields was never personally on the field for any of the three battles. He was wounded in a skirmish the day prior to the battle of Kernstown and turned over field command to Col. Kimball. At Cross Keys, he was in Manassas, and Frémont was the on-scene commander. Bayard's Brigade was temporarily assigned to Frémont at the time and participated in the battle. Prior to Cross Keys, Shields transferred the 7th Indiana, 84th Pennsylvania, 110th Pennsylvania, and 1st West Virginia to Col. Samuel S. Carroll to form the Fourth Brigade. At Port Republic, Shields's Third (Tyler) and Fourth (Carroll) Brigades participated, with Tyler acting as on-scene commander. Shields and his First and Second Brigades were at Luray.

WILLIAMS'S DIVISION	Brig. Gen. S. Williams
First Brigade	Col. Dudley Donnelly
5th Connecticut Infantry	Lt. Col. George D. Chapman
28th New York Infantry	Lt. Col. Edwin F. Brown
46th Pennsylvania Infantry	Col. Joseph F. Knipe
Third Brigade	Col. George Henry Gordon
2nd Massachusetts Infantry	Lt. Col. George L. Andrews
29th Pennsylvania Infantry	Col. John K. Murphy
27th Indiana Infantry	Col. Silas Colgrove
3rd Wisconsin Infantry	Col. Thomas H. Ruger
Cavalry	
1st Michigan Cavalry	Col. Thornton F. Brodhead
Artillery	Capt. Robert B. Hampton
Battery M, 1st New York Light Artillery	Lt. James H. Peabody
Battery F, Pennsylvania Light Artillery	Lt. J. Presley Fleming
Battery B, 4th US Light Artillery	Lt. Franklin B. Crosby
Cavalry Brigade, Independent	Brig. Gen. John P. Hatch
1st Maine Cavalry	Lt. Col. Calvin S. Douty
1st Vermont Cavalry	Col. Charles H. Tompkins
5th New York Cavalry	Col. Othneil DeForest
1st Maryland Cavalry	Lt. Col. Charles Wetschky
1st Michigan Cavalry	Colonel Thornton F. Brodhead
Attached Independent Units	
10th Maine Infantry	Col. George L. Beal
Pennsylvania Zouaves d'Afrique	Capt. Charles H. T. Collis
8th New York Cavalry	Lt. Col. Charles R. Babbitt

Williams's Division participated in the battle of Winchester only.

MOUNTAIN DEPARTMENT	Maj. Gen. John C. Frémont
Milroy's Brigade	Brig. Gen. Robert H. Milroy
12th Ohio Infantry	Col. Carr B. White
25th Ohio Infantry	Lt. Col. William P. Richardson
32nd Ohio Infantry	Lt. Col. Ebenezer H. Swinney
73rd Ohio Infantry	Maj. Richard Long
75th Ohio Infantry	Col. Nathan McLean
2nd West Virginia Infantry	Col. George R. Latham
3rd West Virginia Infantry	Lt. Col. Francis W. Thompson
9th Ohio Battery	Capt. Henry F. Wyman
Schenck's Brigade	Brig. Gen. Robert C. Schenck (on-field commander)
82nd Ohio Infantry	Col. James Cantwell
5th West Virginia Infantry	Col. John L. Ziegler

The Mountain Department participated in the battles of McDowell (Milroy and Schenck only) and Cross Keys.

BLENKER'S DIVISION — Brig. Gen. Louis Blenker

First Brigade	Brig. Gen. Julius Stahel
8th New York Infantry	Col. Francis Wutschel
39th New York Infantry	Col. Frederick G. D'Utassy
41st New York Infantry	Col. Leopold von Gilsa
45th New York Infantry	Col. George von Amsberg
27th Pennsylvania Infantry	Col. Adolphus Buschbeck
2nd Battery, New York Light Artillery	Capt. Louis Schirmer
Battery C, West Virginia Light Artillery	Capt. Frank Buel
Second Brigade	Col. John A. Koltes
29th New York Infantry	Lt. Col. Clemens Soest
68th New York Infantry	Lt. Col. John H. Kleefish
73rd Pennsylvania Infantry	Lt. Col. Gustavus A. Muhlek
13th Battery, New York Light Artillery	Col. Julius Dieckman
Third Brigade	Brig. Gen. Henry Bohlen
54th New York Infantry	Col. Eugene A. Kozley
58th New York Infantry	Col. Wlodzimierz Krzyzanowski
74th Pennsylvania Infantry	Lt. Col. John Hamm
75th Pennsylvania Infantry	Lt. Col. Francis Mahler
Battery I, 1st New York Light Artillery	Capt. Michael Wiedrich
Cavalry	Col. Christian F. Dickel
4th New York Cavalry	Col. Christian F. Dickel

Blenker's Division only participated in the battle of Cross Keys.

ATTACHED INDEPENDENT UNITS

Cluseret's Brigade	Col. Gustave Paul Cluseret
8th West Virginia Infantry	Lt. Col. Lucien Loeser
60th Ohio Infantry	Col. William H. Trimble
Milroy's Brigade	Brig. Gen. Robert H. Milroy
2nd West Virginia Infantry	Maj. James D. Owens
3rd West Virginia Infantry	Lt. Col. Francis W. Thompson
5th West Virginia Infantry	Col. John L. Ziegler
25th Ohio Infantry	Lt. Col. William P. Richardson
1st West Virginia Cavalry	Maj. John A. Kreps
Battery G, West Virginia Light Artillery	Capt. Chatham T. Ewing
Battery I, 1st Ohio Light Artillery	Capt. Henry F. Hayman
12th Battery, Ohio Light Artillery	Capt. Aaron C. Johnson
Schenck's Brigade	Brig. Gen. Robert C. Schenck
32nd Ohio Infantry	Lt. Col. Ebenezer H. Swinney
55th Ohio Infantry	Col. John C. Lee
73rd Ohio Infantry	Col. Orland Smith
75th Ohio Infantry	Col. Nathan McLean
82nd Ohio Infantry	Col. James Cantwell
1st Battalion Connecticut Cavalry	Capt. Erastus Blakeslee
Battery K, 1st Ohio Light Artillery	Capt. William L. DeBeck
Rigby's Battery, Indiana Light Artillery	Capt. Silas S. Rigby
Attached cavalry	
3rd West Virginia Cavalry	Capt. Everton J. Conger
6th Ohio Cavalry	Col. William P. Lloyd

DEPARTMENT OF THE RAPPAHANNOCK
Maj. Gen. Irvin McDowell

SHIELDS'S DIVISION — Brig. Gen. James Shields

Bayard's Brigade	(Temporarily assigned to Frémont's Command) Brig. Gen. Dashiell Bayard
1st New Jersey Cavalry	Lt. Col. Joseph Karge
1st Pennsylvania Cavalry	Col. Owen Jones
13th Pennsylvania Reserves (1st Pennsylvania Rifles) Battalion	Lt. Col. Thomas L. Kane
2nd Battery, Maine Light Artillery	Capt. James A. Hall
Garrison troops	
1st Maryland Infantry	Col. John R. Kenly
29th Pennsylvania Infantry	Lt. Col. Charles Parham
5th New York Cavalry	Maj. Philip G. Vought
Battery E, Pennsylvania Light Artillery	Lt. Charles A. Atwell
Pioneer Company	Capt. William H. H. Mapes

OPPOSING PLANS

In his *Narrative*, General Joseph E. Johnston stated of First Manassas, "the Confederate Army was more disorganized by victory than that of the United States by defeat." (LOC)

The success of the Confederate forces at the battle of Manassas convinced many of the Southern volunteers that the objectives of the war had been accomplished, that the South was secure from further invasion, and they had done all that their country expected of them. President Davis and his military advisors knew otherwise and faced the daunting task of consolidating their victory and preparing for the longer war.

The Federal Army may have been temporarily disrupted by their defeat, but the North was not yet ready to concede anything to the South, and was still dictating the overall direction of the war. In May 1861, Lt. Gen. Scott had proposed his "Anaconda Plan," calling for a blockade of all Southern ports and a simultaneous advance down the Mississippi River to cut the Confederacy in two and persuade the anti-Secessionists in the Southern States to rise up and reclaim their government. The plan was derided by the Northern firebrands, who thought it too passive and, particularly after Bull Run, demanded an all-out war effort by the North.

Lincoln also desperately wanted action, but first had to repair his shattered army. He turned to Maj. Gen. McClellan, who was a superb organizer who transformed the Union Army. His goal was to instill a confidence in that army that would enable it to heed the North's battle cry, "On to Richmond." Where he fell short was in leading his troops in the field.

Despite the Union commander's faults, Johnston and Davis knew he would take the field eventually. A conference of the senior leadership of the Confederate Army at the end of September had persuaded Davis that a shortage of the basic requirements of an army, namely men and equipment, dictated a primarily defensive stance against the North, at least initially. Johnston felt that "the next important service of that army would be near the end of October, against the invasion of a much greater Federal army" than the one they'd fought in July.

As the months passed with nothing more than a series of small blunders by the North, like the badly bungled affair at Ball's Bluff which led to Scott's retirement, the preparatory actions continued. Jackson established his headquarters at Winchester on November 4. As the left wing of Johnston's department his duties were straightforward: keep an eye on the enemy in the region, keep open the lines of communication with Johnston, and be ready to join the main army, as he had the previous summer, when Union forces began to advance.

Jackson yearned to go on the offensive. In October 1861 he proposed an invasion of Pennsylvania. "McClellan," he said, "with his army of recruits, will not attempt to come out against us this autumn. If we remain inactive they will have the advantage over us next spring." He concluded, "We ought to invade their country now, and not wait for them to make the necessary preparations to invade ours." When his plan to "force the people of the North to understand what it will cost them to hold the South in the Union at the bayonet's point," was disapproved, he submitted a second proposal to advance on the Federal garrison at Romney in northwestern Virginia. This, Davis was willing to allow.

As Jackson was launching his Romney Expedition on January 1, 1862, Johnston was reporting an effective total of 57,337 troops within the Department of Northern Virginia. Of those, 10,241 were in the Valley District. Coincidentally, McClellan was reporting 183,507 present for duty in the Army of the Potomac, of which 16,000 were with Banks's Division, responsible for the Shenandoah Valley region. Any disparity in troop strength did little to dissuade Jackson. He understood that the bulk of the Union troops was north of the Potomac, but the opportunity to attack the isolated garrison of 5,000 men under Brig. Gen. Benjamin F. Kelley at Romney was too good an opportunity to miss.

"I find myself in a new & strange position here – Presdt, Cabinet, Genl Scott & all deferring to me." McClellan to his wife Mary Ellen, July 27, 1861. (LOC)

Guarding the Road to Winchester. Occupied by Captain Wallace of the Fourth Ohio Regiment. under Brigadier Genl Kelley Command.

In the fall of 1861, Jackson proposed an invasion of the North through Romney, occupied by the 4th Ohio Infantry. From northwest Virginia, he would join with Johnston to take Philadelphia. (LOC)

McClellan's delays were ridiculed in the Northern press. This cartoon shows him with Uncle Sam before a playbill announcing, "Every day this week, Onward to Richmond, by a select company of star Generals." (LOC)

Kelley's men withdrew as Jackson approached. The weather was brutal and Jackson decided upon capturing the town to return to Winchester, leaving a detachment under Brig. Gen. William W. Loring, behind. He had hardly returned to the Valley when he received a letter from Secretary of War Judah P. Benjamin. "Our news indicates that a movement is making to cut off General Loring's command; order him back immediately."

As soon as Jackson had left Romney, the officers under Loring had filed a complaint through government civilian channels, with Loring's approval, of Jackson's handling of the Romney expedition. They maintained that they had been poorly used, and Romney itself held little strategic value. Jackson did as he was directed and then submitted his resignation. "With such interference in my command I cannot expect to be of much service in the field." The fact that the order had come, not from his military superior General Johnston but directly from the civilian Secretary of War, induced Jackson to believe that his judgment was being called into question.

Jackson wrote to Johnston and Virginia governor John Letcher explaining his actions. Both men were well aware of Jackson's abilities and persuaded him to withdraw his request. A potential crisis was averted, but the issue of civilian control of the military was one that would affect more than one officer during the Civil War.

McClellan had submitted his original plan of operations for all Union forces on August 4, 1861. He proposed an advance on all fronts, with particular emphasis on Nashville and Richmond, supported by operations down the Mississippi. Initially, Lincoln waited patiently for McClellan to put his plan into action. As fall dragged into winter, the President became increasingly anxious for McClellan to do something, anything. McClellan reassured him that he was getting close, but in December he fell ill and it wasn't until mid-January that he was again ready to take up the issue of going on the offensive.

On January 20 Edwin M. Stanton was appointed Secretary of War in place of Simon Cameron. One of Stanton's first acts was to direct McClellan to take immediate steps to reopen the Baltimore and Ohio Railroad, which

Saturday & Sunday
24 & 25 May 2014

KINGS X AND KING & COUNTRY
PROUDLY PRESENT

THE 2014 TEXAS TOY SOLDIER SHOW
SAN ANTONIO TX.

SAN ANTONIO is where you will find AMERICA's fastest-growing Toy Soldier Show! Our **2-Day Event** brings together the *top toy soldier dealers, manufacturers* and *collectors* from all over the world right into the heart of the *Lone Star State...*

You can see all kind[s] great toy soldiers military miniatures to sui[t] kinds of tastes... *and bud[gets]* **PLUS** we have *living his[tory] reenactors... live vintage mu[sic]* a *Saturday Night Dinne[r] Symposium...* and a *Sp[ecial] Guest!!!* All of this and m[uch] much more within a sto[ne's] throw from the *legendary Al[amo]*

Come on down to see[...]

SHOW TIMES

SATURDAY	SUNDAY
10:00 am ~ 5:00 pm	11:00 am ~ 3:00 pm

MENGER
H O T E L

204 Alamo Plaza, San Antonio, Texas

For more details and information about the show please visit our we[bsite]
at www.kingsx.com or call KingsX at 210-226-7000.

ran through the northern end of the Shenandoah Valley, and to readdress his plan for attacking Richmond. McClellan proposed sending his army "down the Chesapeake, up the Rappahannock to Urbana, and across land to the terminus of the railroad on the York River," whereas Lincoln proposed a more direct overland attack.

Lincoln eventually complied with McClellan's desires, with one critical caveat, that "no change of the base of operations of the Army of the Potomac shall be made without leaving in and about Washington such a force as, in the opinion of the General-in-Chief and the commanders of army corps, shall leave said city entirely secure." In Lincoln's mind, the security of Washington depended on leaving McDowell's Corps within supporting distance of any enemy action against the Capital. McClellan was adamant that the success of his Peninsula campaign hinged on a simultaneous advance of his own forces up the Peninsula with McDowell's advance overland via Fredericksburg.

At the end of February, McClellan traveled to Harper's Ferry to observe Banks's advance into Virginia to secure the reopening of the railroad. Johnston and Davis told Jackson that it was his job to do everything that Lincoln and McClellan most feared – tie up Union troops in the Valley, convince Lincoln to keep McDowell where he was, and ultimately slip away to join Johnston at Richmond and attack McClellan.

McDowell took the brunt of criticism for the Bull Run disaster. During the Valley campaign he became entangled in a tug-of-war between Lincoln and McClellan for the use of his corps. (LOC)

31

THE CAMPAIGN

OPENING MOVES

On February 26, 1862, after considerable effort, a 1,300ft makeshift pontoon bridge was thrown across the Potomac River at Harper's Ferry and Maj. Gen. Nathaniel Banks's Division of McClellan's Army of the Potomac crossed into Virginia. By nightfall, 8,500 infantry, 18 guns, and two squadrons of cavalry were advancing on Charlestown.

As McClellan accompanied Banks they discussed the possibility of attacking Winchester. With the Confederacy seemingly on the defensive, "This is a favorable opportunity," Banks had suggested on the 23rd. "The roads to Winchester are turnpikes and in tolerable condition. The enemy is weak, demoralized, and depressed." McClellan was concerned about being able to adequately supply his troops until a permanent bridge could be completed across the Potomac. "I cannot, as things are now, be sure of my supplies for the force necessary to seize Winchester," he told Secretary Stanton. In the meantime, they would move deliberately. Banks's first objective was to occupy a line some 22 miles north of Winchester to oversee the reconstruction of the Baltimore and Ohio Railroad, a vital lifeline for supplies and information which had suffered widespread destruction, mostly by Southern cavalry and militia, the previous summer.

McClellan preferred the 31ft-long, flat-bottomed wooden pontoons of the "French" design to the Goodyear Company's 1840 India-rubber design. This sketch depicts the 1,300ft bridge that enabled Banks to invade the Valley. (LOC)

Banks arrived in Charlestown, 7 miles from Harper's Ferry, on February 28. His reported strength was now up to 16,801 officers and men present for duty. Brigadier-General John Sedgwick's Division was at Harper's Ferry with another 11,470, and Brig. Gen. Frederick W. Lander was in supporting distance, 40 miles northwest, with 15,731. Lander was ordered to occupy Martinsburg, oversee the reconstruction of the railroad to there, and then move to Bunker Hill 15 miles north of Winchester. Jackson could feel the noose tightening. On March 3, he sent a note to Johnston at Centreville outlining his plan to withdraw to New Market. There he would have the choice of continuing up the Valley to Staunton, "if the enemy should move in that direction," or take, in his mind, the less attractive option of leaving the Valley altogether.

In the end, the decision was made for him. Everyone knew that McClellan was going to march eventually, they just didn't know how or when. When unusual activity was noted in the Federal camps on the Maryland side of the Potomac on March 5, Johnston gave the order to evacuate the Centreville Line and retire to the fieldworks already prepared south of the Rappahannock River. Johnston wrote to Jackson instructing him to "delay the enemy as long as you can." Jackson replied that he would "greatly desire to hold this place [Winchester] so far as may be consistent with your views and plans."

When McClellan learned that Johnston was abandoning Centreville, he directed Banks to move on Winchester. On March 12 lead elements of Banks's Corps entered the town, which Jackson had reluctantly abandoned the night before. McClellan's instructions were for Banks to hold himself in readiness to move with the whole or part of his force on Manassas. Clearly, Banks's time in the Valley was meant to be of short duration.

The effect of Johnston's move to his new, fortified line, while strengthening his overall defenses, uncovered the Manassas Gap Railroad and effectively isolated Jackson. Any other commander may have seen this as a weakening of his position, and Jackson hoped that Banks would also see things that way and expose himself to attack.

The total amount of repair work facing the railroad reconstruction crews in 1862 included 26 bridges like this one (127 spans with a total length of 4,713ft), 102 miles of telegraph line and a pair of water stations. (LOC)

Banks's first objective upon entering Virginia was Charlestown. His orders were to oversee the reconstruction of the railroad while keeping an eye on Jackson. (LOC)

Major battles, March to June 1862

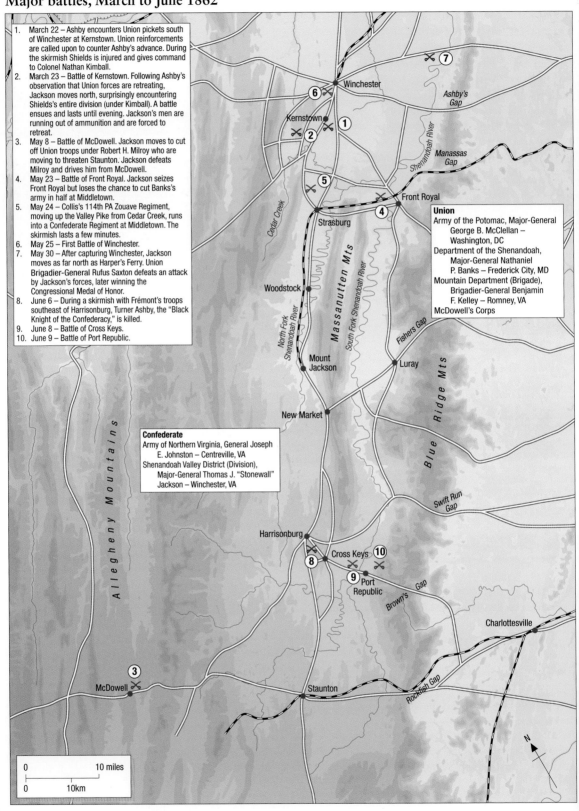

1. March 22 – Ashby encounters Union pickets south of Winchester at Kernstown. Union reinforcements are called upon to counter Ashby's advance. During the skirmish Shields is injured and gives command to Colonel Nathan Kimball.
2. March 23 – Battle of Kernstown. Following Ashby's observation that Union forces are retreating, Jackson moves north, surprisingly encountering Shields's entire division (under Kimball). A battle ensues and lasts until evening. Jackson's men are running out of ammunition and are forced to retreat.
3. May 8 – Battle of McDowell. Jackson moves to cut off Union troops under Robert H. Milroy who are moving to threaten Staunton. Jackson defeats Milroy and drives him from McDowell.
4. May 23 – Battle of Front Royal. Jackson seizes Front Royal but loses the chance to cut Banks's army in half at Middletown.
5. May 24 – Collis's 114th PA Zouave Regiment, moving up the Valley Pike from Cedar Creek, runs into a Confederate Regiment at Middletown. The skirmish lasts a few minutes.
6. May 25 – First Battle of Winchester.
7. May 30 – After capturing Winchester, Jackson moves as far north as Harper's Ferry. Union Brigadier-General Rufus Saxton defeats an attack by Jackson's forces, later winning the Congressional Medal of Honor.
8. June 6 – During a skirmish with Frémont's troops southeast of Harrisonburg, Turner Ashby, the "Black Knight of the Confederacy," is killed.
9. June 8 – Battle of Cross Keys.
10. June 9 – Battle of Port Republic.

Union
Army of the Potomac, Major-General George B. McClellan – Washington, DC
Department of the Shenandoah, Major-General Nathaniel P. Banks – Frederick City, MD
Mountain Department (Brigade), Brigadier-General Benjamin F. Kelley – Romney, VA
McDowell's Corps

Confederate
Army of Northern Virginia, General Joseph E. Johnston – Centreville, VA
Shenandoah Valley District (Division), Major-General Thomas J. "Stonewall" Jackson – Winchester, VA

No sooner had Banks marched into Winchester than his units were being redirected. Brigadier-General James Sedgwick was ordered to return with his division to Harper's Ferry where he would be detached from Banks's newly designated V Corps and sent on to Centreville. Banks himself was then directed to leave Brig. Gen. James Shields's Division at Winchester and travel to Washington for a conference with McClellan. McClellan

Federal troops discovered that the cannons they believed Johnston's retreating army left behind at Centreville were actually painted logs, known as Quaker Guns, as depicted in this photo. (LOC)

had finally started to move his forces to the Peninsula on the 14th, but he expressed his concern for a "pernicious" move made by the President to reorganize the Army.

On March 11, Lincoln removed McClellan from his position as General-in-Chief, and from the responsibility of commanding anything other than the Army of the Potomac, in order to give his full attention to the Peninsula Campaign. McClellan believed that the attack on the Confederate capital should be the principal objective of the Federal Army, and all other operations were subordinate to it. He wanted Banks to leave the Valley and command his Corps from Manassas Junction, deeming it adequate that, "something like two regiments of cavalry should be left in that vicinity to occupy Winchester." Lincoln was skeptical that Jackson was no longer a threat and remained alert for any indication of enemy activity that could threaten Washington.

Over the next ten days a flurry of activity occurred in the Valley as McClellan reported:

> On the 13th, the mass of Banks's Corps was concentrated in the immediate vicinity of Winchester, the enemy being in the rear of Strasburg. On the 19th General Shields occupied Strasburg, driving the enemy 20 miles south to Mount Jackson. On the 20th the first division of Banks's Corps commenced its movement towards Manassas, in compliance with my letter of instruction. Jackson probably received information of this movement and supposed that no force of any consequence was left in the vicinity of Winchester.

Jackson was indeed receiving information on the enemy's movements. His cavalry commander Col. Turner Ashby was shadowing the Federal troops, and Jackson had his own spies gathering information. McClellan, finally operating from the Peninsula, was the focus of attention for both sides. In his March 14 address to his troops, he stated, "the moment for action had arrived, and I know that I can trust in you to save our country," while Confederate forces desperately organized defensive positions Jackson, with his force of 5,000 men isolated in the Valley, was determined to do anything he could he upset the Federal plan.

THE FIRST BATTLE OF KERNSTOWN, MARCH 23

Brigadier-General James Shields, commanding Banks's Second Division, was deemed to have sufficient force to defend against anything Jackson might do. He returned to Winchester on March 20 to again guard the railroad and the canal, and, according to his report, "draw (Jackson) from his position and supporting force, if possible." Banks was ordered to proceed with Brig. Gen. Alpheus S. Williams's First Division to Centreville and establish his headquarters at Manassas Junction.

If the intent was to draw Jackson north, it worked. On March 21 Ashby sent word to Jackson that the enemy was retreating. Reports from his own spies supported the statements from the townspeople of Winchester that a large Federal wagon train was on the road to Castlemans Ferry on the Shenandoah – Banks was headed east. Jackson immediately put his men on the march.

At about 4pm in the afternoon of the 22nd, Ashby encountered Union pickets from the 1st Michigan Cavalry about a mile south of Winchester, near the tiny village of Kernstown, and a skirmish ensued. Shields immediately summoned reinforcements, but only enough to counter Ashby's advance. In his report on the battle, Shields stated that he "pushed forward one brigade and two batteries of artillery to drive back the enemy, but to keep him deceived as to our strength."

Ashby took the bait. "Having followed the enemy in his hasty retreat from Strasburg on Saturday evening, I learned that they had orders to march in the direction of Harper's Ferry." Ashby was convinced that less than 3,000 of Shields's troops remained. In fact, Shields had three times that many.

During the skirmish Shields was injured by a shell fragment and had to turn over field command to Col. Nathan Kimball, commander of the First Brigade. Kimball ordered a general advance at twilight and Federal artillery fire forced Ashby to pull back. Banks, who was still at Winchester, went to bed believing that there was still no threat from Jackson's main force, and intended to leave for Manassas in the morning.

Kimball followed his defeat of Lee at Cheat Mountain with his victory over Jackson at Kernstown, making him the only Union general to defeat both Confederate generals during the war. (LOC)

Kimball's Brigade settled in for the night in the vicinity of Pritchard's Farm, half a mile north of Kernstown. Colonel Jeremiah C. Sullivan encamped the Second Brigade near Hillman's tollgate on the Valley Pike just to the north, while Col. Erastus B. Tyler and the Third Brigade remained north of Winchester. For his part, Jackson was already at Strasburg, 16 miles south of Kernstown. At dawn the next day he continued the march and "learned from a source which had been remarkable for its reliability that the enemy's infantry force at Winchester did not exceed four regiments."

On the morning of Sunday, March 23, at about 9am, Ashby again advanced along the Valley Pike and engaged Sullivan's skirmish line on rising ground just north of Kernstown. The firing from Ashby's Blakely gun did little more than alert Kimball to his presence. Kimball had placed ten rifled guns, including the six 10-pdr Parrotts of Capt. Joseph Clark's Battery E, 4th US Artillery, on Pritchard's Hill, which had a commanding view of the area from the west of the Pike. Kimball's own First Brigade supported the guns while Tyler's Third Brigade remained out of sight to the rear. Ashby's attempts to turn the Union left flank were repeatedly repulsed.

By 1pm, Jackson's three brigades arrived on the field after completing a march of over 35 miles in two days. His initial inclination was to allow the men to rest for the night. His troops were tired from the march, and he didn't want to fight on a Sunday. Once he had a chance to observe the situation he quickly changed his mind. "Ascertaining that the Federals had a position from which our forces could be seen, I concluded that it would be dangerous to postpone the attack until the next day, as reinforcements might be brought up during the night."

Noting the strength of the Union position, Jackson attempted to counter the artillery on Pritchard's Hill by assaulting the Union right. About 1.30pm in the afternoon, after leaving Ashby to demonstrate along the Valley Pike, he ordered his Third Brigade commander Col. Samuel V. Fulkerson, supported by Brig. Gen.

Richard B. Garnett's Stonewall Brigade, to "turn a battery of the enemy, which had opened fire upon us from a commanding hill across the fields in my front."

Fulkerson led the 37th Virginia Infantry toward the enemy's position. Slowed by the condition of the ground and the firing of the Union guns, they were pushed to the left. By 2.15pm "under a fire that might well have made veterans quail," Fulkerson's regiment had advanced about half a mile. They took position in a hollow 600 yards west of Pritchard's Hill. Garnett, attempting to follow, sheltered his brigade another 600 yards to the south and went forward personally to find Fulkerson. The two encountered each other just south of Fulkerson's position, and Fulkerson reported his position to Jackson.

"I came upon the forces remaining in Winchester within a mile of that place and became satisfied that he had but four regiments." Ashby to Jackson on the eve of the battle of Kernstown. (LOC)

With the 37th Virginia Infantry in the lead, Fulkerson's troops tore down a plank fence and advanced across the marshy fields directly in front of the enemy's position on Pritchard's Hill. (Author's collection)

Note: Gridlines are shown at intervals of 1km (0.62 mile)

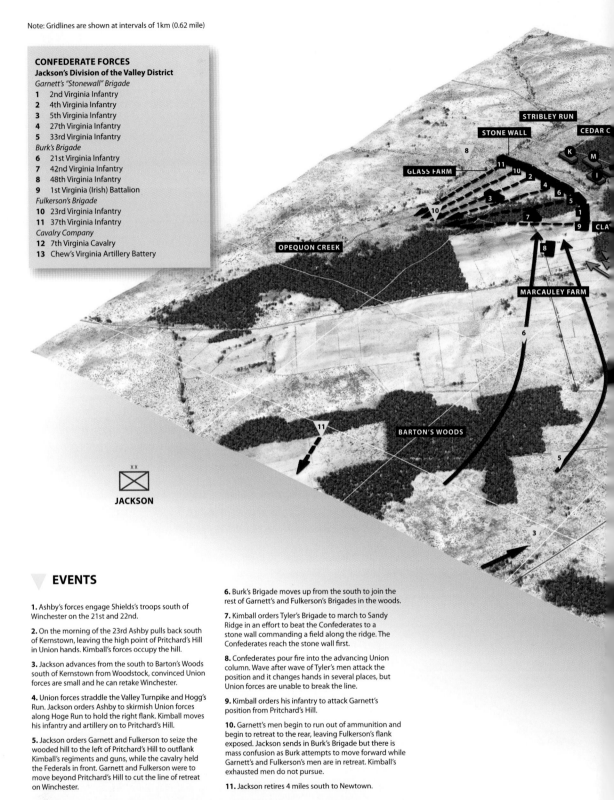

CONFEDERATE FORCES
Jackson's Division of the Valley District
Garnett's "Stonewall" Brigade
1   2nd Virginia Infantry
2   4th Virginia Infantry
3   5th Virginia Infantry
4   27th Virginia Infantry
5   33rd Virginia Infantry
Burk's Brigade
6   21st Virginia Infantry
7   42nd Virginia Infantry
8   48th Virginia Infantry
9   1st Virginia (Irish) Battalion
Fulkerson's Brigade
10 23rd Virginia Infantry
11 37th Virginia Infantry
Cavalry Company
12 7th Virginia Cavalry
13 Chew's Virginia Artillery Battery

JACKSON

EVENTS

1. Ashby's forces engage Shields's troops south of Winchester on the 21st and 22nd.

2. On the morning of the 23rd Ashby pulls back south of Kernstown, leaving the high point of Pritchard's Hill in Union hands. Kimball's forces occupy the hill.

3. Jackson advances from the south to Barton's Woods south of Kernstown, convinced Union forces are small and he can retake Winchester.

4. Union forces straddle the Valley Turnpike and Hogg's Run. Jackson orders Ashby to skirmish Union forces along Hoge Run to hold the right flank. Kimball moves his infantry and artillery on to Pritchard's Hill.

5. Jackson orders Garnett and Fulkerson to seize the wooded hill to the left of Pritchard's Hill to outflank Kimball's regiments and guns, while the cavalry held the Federals in front. Garnett and Fulkerson were to move beyond Pritchard's Hill to cut the line of retreat on Winchester.

6. Burk's Brigade moves up from the south to join the rest of Garnett's and Fulkerson's Brigades in the woods.

7. Kimball orders Tyler's Brigade to march to Sandy Ridge in an effort to beat the Confederates to a stone wall commanding a field along the ridge. The Confederates reach the stone wall first.

8. Confederates pour fire into the advancing Union column. Wave after wave of Tyler's men attack the position and it changes hands in several places, but Union forces are unable to break the line.

9. Kimball orders his infantry to attack Garnett's position from Pritchard's Hill.

10. Garnett's men begin to run out of ammunition and begin to retreat to the rear, leaving Fulkerson's flank exposed. Jackson sends in Burk's Brigade but there is mass confusion as Burk attempts to move forward while Garnett's and Fulkerson's men are in retreat. Kimball's exhausted men do not pursue.

11. Jackson retires 4 miles south to Newtown.

THE BATTLE OF KERNSTOWN, MARCH 23, 1862
Jackson's Division attacks Shields's Division, 9am to 7pm

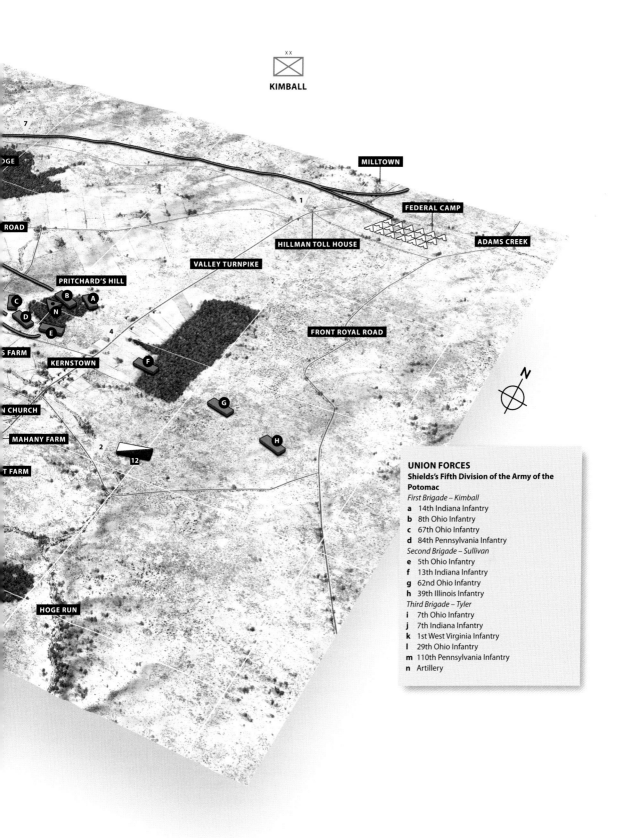

XX
KIMBALL

7

MILLTOWN

1

FEDERAL CAMP

ROAD

OGE

HILLMAN TOLL HOUSE

ADAMS CREEK

VALLEY TURNPIKE

PRITCHARD'S HILL

C
D
B
A
N
E

FARM

4

FRONT ROYAL ROAD

KERNSTOWN

F

N CHURCH

G

MAHANY FARM

2

H

T FARM

12

HOGE RUN

UNION FORCES
Shields's Fifth Division of the Army of the Potomac
First Brigade – Kimball
a 14th Indiana Infantry
b 8th Ohio Infantry
c 67th Ohio Infantry
d 84th Pennsylvania Infantry
Second Brigade – Sullivan
e 5th Ohio Infantry
f 13th Indiana Infantry
g 62nd Ohio Infantry
h 39th Illinois Infantry
Third Brigade – Tyler
i 7th Ohio Infantry
j 7th Indiana Infantry
k 1st West Virginia Infantry
l 29th Ohio Infantry
m 110th Pennsylvania Infantry
n Artillery

Jackson began directing his units to the top of Sandy Ridge, less than a mile west of Pritchard's Hill. The ridge soon became the focus of the late afternoon's battle. (Author's collection)

Jackson was now focusing his attention on Sandy Ridge, a rise of ground less than a mile west of Pritchard's Hill across the Middle Road. He initially directed elements of the Rockbridge Artillery to occupy the heights and counter the fire of the Union guns. Kimball, observing the pressure on his right, ordered the 84th Pennsylvania and 5th and 67th Ohio Infantry west toward the ridge.

Fulkerson continued moving to his left and into a tract of woods west of the Middle Road near the base of Sandy Ridge. Garnett, with the 33rd Virginia Infantry, was 600 yards further south, but both men had lost contact with Jackson. Jackson sent one of his aides, Lt. Sandie Pendleton, to a high point on the ridge where he had a clear view of Pritchard's Hill to the west. Pendleton reported some 10,000 enemy troops in his front. "We are in for it," Jackson stated.

At 3pm the two long-range rifled guns of the Rockbridge Artillery opened fire from Sandy Ridge. Kimball sent word to Col. Tyler "to move to the right to gain the flank of the enemy, and charge them through the wood to their batteries posted on the hill." Just before 4pm the first Union skirmishers from the 7th Ohio Infantry encountered a line of Confederate skirmishers 300 yards north of a chest-high stone wall, running east–west across the ridge. Barely ten minutes earlier the 27th Virginia Infantry had arrived at the wall that would become the center of the late afternoon's battle.

Jackson was now feeding his units piecemeal to the top of the ridge. The 21st Virginia Infantry came in to the right of the 27th. Tyler's 1st West Virginia Infantry charged to an undefended portion of the wall left of the 27th, only to be met by the 23rd and 37th Virginia Infantry. Seemingly just in time, Fulkerson had run to the sound of the guns, as had Garnett with the 33rd, followed by the 4th Virginia Infantry. To the north, the remainder of Tyler's Brigade – the 7th Indiana Infantry, 110th Pennsylvania Infantry, 29th Ohio Infantry, along with Copeland's 1st Michigan Cavalry – had also entered the fight.

Fighting raged at the wall for nearly an hour, when Kimball ordered the 8th Ohio Infantry, which had been engaged west of Pritchard's Hill along the Middle Road throughout the afternoon, forward up the ridge, followed over the next hour by the 13th and 14th Indiana Infantry, and the remaining units of his brigade. The 8th Ohio Infantry struck the 1st and 2nd Virginia Infantry at a right angle to the wall.

Jackson was beginning to feel the pressure of the enemy's reinforcements, and was also beginning to wonder if the best he could hope for was a stalemate. He had only three unengaged units left and twilight was fast approaching. "From near 5 to 6:30 p.m. there was almost a continuous roar of musketry. The enemy's repulsed regiments were replaced by fresh ones from his large reserve. As the ammunition of some of our men became exhausted noble instances were seen of their borrowing from their comrades, by whose sides they continued to fight, as though resolved to die rather than give way."

"The fire of the enemy was poured in upon us from behind a stone wall with terrible affect," stated Union General Erastus Tyler. This sketch shows the combined Union charge that routed the Rebels. (LOC)

On the Union side Tyler was fighting for every inch when the assault of the men of Kimball's Brigade broke the Confederate right. "The timely arrival of the Fourteenth Indiana, Lieutenant-Colonel Harrow, in this unequal contest was of immense service, followed as they were soon after by the Eighty-fourth Pennsylvania, Colonel Murray; Thirteenth Indiana, Lieutenant-Colonel Foster, and still later by the Sixty-seventh, Lieutenant-Colonel Voris, and Fifth Ohio, Lieutenant-Colonel Patrick, routing the enemy just as twilight was fading into night."

Just after 6pm, as Jackson was furiously trying to rush his dwindling reinforcements to the line, he became aware of Garnett's men falling back. Brigadier-General Garnett maintained that his men were running out of ammunition and could no longer hold their position. He ordered the 21st Virginia Infantry to withdraw, followed by the Irish Battalion. As the right flank gave way, Fulkerson had no choice but to follow suit. "Though our troops were fighting under great disadvantages, I regret that General Garnett should have given the order to fall back," Jackson wrote, "as otherwise the enemy's advance would at least have been retarded."

By 7pm Union troops had cleared the stone wall and the last Confederate units withdrew. Kimball was promoted to brigadier-general for his victory. (Author's collection)

It was all over by 7pm as the Union troops cleared the stone wall and Jackson was forced to abandon the field. "Leaving Ashby in front, the remainder of my command fell back on its wagons and bivouacked for the night," Jackson reported. Kimball, his men equally exhausted, and with darkness falling, declined to pursue.

FROM KERNSTOWN TO MCDOWELL, MARCH 24–MAY 7

After the battle, Jackson and Shields submitted their respective reports. Considering that the Union forces had prevailed in their first major contest with Jackson, the opinions of the two opposing commanders were definitely a portent of the future. Shields expressed confidence that he had dealt a severe blow to the enemy: "Jackson, with his supposed invincible 'Stonewall Brigade' and the accompanying brigades, much to their mortification and discomfiture were compelled by this terrific fire to fall back in disorder upon their reserve." But he remained cautious. "Though the battle had been won," he wrote, "still I could not have believed that Jackson would have hazarded a decisive engagement, so far from the main body; so, to be prepared for such a contingency, I set to work during the night to bring together all the troops within my reach."

Banks was at Harper's Ferry when he received word of the battle. He immediately turned around and also ordered Williams's Division back to Winchester. McClellan, on receiving Banks's report, concurred with his decision to recall the scattered elements of his command and encouraged him to press and defeat Jackson, reminding him that the ultimate objective must continue to be an eventual move to Manassas.

Jackson expressed much greater confidence. Although Kernstown may have been a tactical defeat, he had achieved a strategic victory. "Though Winchester was not recovered, yet the more important object for the present, that of calling back troops that were leaving the valley, and thus preventing a junction of Banks's command with other forces, was accomplished. I feel justified in saying," he wrote, "that though the battlefield is in the possession of the enemy, yet the most essential fruits of the victory are ours." Events over the next few months would strongly support his opinion.

Fort Richardson, pictured here, was one of many under the command of Brig. Gen. James Wadsworth, who expressed his grave concern for his ability to defend the Federal Capital in the spring of 1862. (LOC)

As both sides were attempting to determine what the battle at Kernstown really meant, Brig. Gen. James S. Wadsworth, commander of the Military District of Washington, sent a message to President Lincoln. "In regard to the character and efficiency of the troops under my command, I have to state that nearly all the force is new and imperfectly disciplined; that several of the regiments are in a very disorganized condition." As the official responsible for the defense of the Federal capital he then expressed his greatest concern: "I deem it my duty to state that, looking at the numerical strength and character of the force under my command, it is, in my judgment, entirely inadequate to, and unfit for, the important duty to which it is assigned."

This was exactly the situation that Lincoln most feared. He fired off a dispatch to McClellan, admonishing him for his failure to adequately safeguard Washington as he had promised to do. "I do not forget that I was satisfied with your arrangements to leave Banks at Manassas Junction, but when that arrangement was broken up and nothing was substituted for it of course I was not satisfied," Lincoln stated on April 9. He continued, "I was constrained to substitute something for it myself." And substitute he did.

Lincoln had previously decided to transfer the 9,000 men of Brig. Gen. Louis Blenker's division from McClellan to Maj. Gen. John C. Frémont's Mountain Department at Wheeling, Virginia. Now, he redesignated McDowell's 37,000-man corps as an independent command to remain at Manassas rather than allowing it to proceed to the Peninsula. Finally, Banks was also withdrawn from McClellan's control and directed to defend the Valley, his command redesignated as the Department of the Shenandoah.

"Jackson has been seen moving toward Port Republic, and… his intention may possibly be to join Johnson and attack you." Frémont to Milroy, May 4, 1862. (LOC)

McClellan was incensed at the loss of 46,000 troops from his planned invasion force and declared that the success of the Federal cause was now imperiled. In a letter to his wife he stated, "I have raised an awful row about McDowell's Corps – & have I think rather scared the authorities that be. The Presdt very coolly telegraphed me yesterday that he thought I had better break the enemy's lines at once! I was much tempted to reply that he had better come & do it himself."

Banks took up the pursuit of Jackson at daybreak on March 24, but his uncertainty as to the exact size of the army he was chasing made him wary. Estimates ran as high as 15,000 men, and rumors abounded of Jackson being reinforced by Maj. Gen. James Longstreet, who was currently supporting Johnston on the Peninsula. Banks moved cautiously. He reached Strasburg on the 25th and pushed his cavalry in the direction of Woodstock. On the night of the 26th, Federal outposts were established at Tom's Brook 17 miles from Kernstown, with Ashby's cavalry watching them from the opposite bank. Jackson left Burks's Brigade at Woodstock and continued on to Mount Jackson. Banks remained virtually stationary for the next three weeks while he resupplied his army and pondered his next move.

The pause enabled Jackson to make a number of decisions that would have major implications for the remainder of the campaign. For some time, he had been concerned with the conduct, discipline, and independence of Ashby's cavalry. Within the Confederate army, independent cavalry companies were being reorganized into regiments and assigned to the infantry commanders. Jackson made Ashby's 21 cavalry companies into two regiments assigned to Charles S. Winder, the newly designated commander of the Stonewall Brigade, and William B. Taliaferro, the new commander of the Third Brigade. Winder had been promoted to brigadier-general on March 1 and replaced Garnett, who had been arrested by Jackson for retreating without orders at Kernstown. Ashby was outraged by Jackson's interference with his organization and submitted his resignation. Into the fray stepped Winder who acted as a mediator. Jackson and Ashby talked and the next day the two cavalry regiments remained assigned to the infantry commanders, but were "detailed" to Ashby for his use.

Jackson's concern for discipline also extended to his infantry, and he spent considerable time in ensuring that his men were properly drilled. The experience of marching over 35 miles in two days and then being forced to immediately go into battle at Kernstown had made a major impression on him. He knew that he couldn't afford to lose a sizeable portion of his manpower to straggling, particularly when confronted by a numerically superior foe, and he vowed not to let it happen again. His men began a steady regimen of drill and marching.

Finally, Jackson turned his attention to the topology of the Valley. He directed Capt. Jedediah Hotchkiss "to make me a map of the Valley, from Harper's Ferry to Lexington, showing all the points of offense and defense." Included would be tables showing the mileage between the significant features of the Valley. Jackson's detailed knowledge of the region in which he operated would be instrumental to his success in the coming months.

On April 16 a company of Ashby's cavalry was surprised and captured at Columbia Furnace, 7 miles from Mount Jackson, and the period of rest came to an end. Early on the morning of the 17th Banks sent Col. Samuel Carroll's

"I want you to make me a map of the Valley, from Harper's Ferry to Lexington, showing all the points of offence and defence in those places." Jackson to Jedediah Hotchkiss, March 26, 1862. (LOC)

Brigade of Shields's Division by a side road to the rear of Mount Jackson, while Kimball, followed by Williams, advanced up the Pike. Jackson's men burned the railway station at Mount Jackson and fell back southwards while the Federal cavalry seized New Market.

Jackson became increasingly concerned for his lines of communication. Massanutten Mountain, rising to nearly 2,700ft, bisects the Shenandoah Valley just east of Strasburg with one pass, New Market Gap, leading into the Luray Valley further to the east. If Banks moved in that direction and took control of Swift Run Gap across the Blue Ridge, Jackson would be cut off from Johnston and, more importantly, from Richard S. Ewell's 8,500-man division at Brandy Station, which had been directed by Johnston to cooperate with Jackson.

Jackson passed through Harrisonburg, 25 miles south of Mount Jackson, crossed the Shenandoah at Conrad's Store, and went into camp at Elk Run Valley at the entrance to Swift Run Gap. Banks, following at his usual deliberate pace, fully occupied New Market on the 19th; crossed Massanutten Mountain to seize the two bridges across the south fork of the Shenandoah River in the Luray Valley; and occupied Harrisonburg on the 22nd. Although congratulated by the Secretary of War for his "brilliant and successful operations," Banks's brigades were becoming increasingly spread out, but he reported, "Jackson has abandoned the valley of Virginia permanently, en route for Gordonsville, by the way of the mountains."

"This man Jackson is certainly a crazy fool, an idiot." Ewell to Colonel Thomas Munford, May 1862. (LOC)

Thirty miles south of Harrisonburg was Staunton, which, for Johnston and the Confederate leadership, was the key to the Southern Valley. There, the Virginia and Tennessee Railroad, running from Richmond to Chattanooga, was a major supply route to the west. Federal control of Staunton would be a severe blow to the South.

The previous December, some 50 miles west of Staunton, Confederate Brig. Gen. Edward Johnson with a small division of 2,800 men had fought off an attack by Union Brig. Gen. Robert H. Milroy's Brigade at the battle of Allegheny Mountain. Johnson earned the nickname "Allegheny" for his efforts there, and remained at Camp Allegheny throughout the winter. But by April 20, feeling threatened by Banks's advance and increasing pressure from Frémont on the far side of the Shenandoah Mountains, he withdrew to West View, 7 miles west of Staunton.

"Too bad to be wounded in the first fight; I would not have cared after some of the big battles." Allegheny Johnson to Hotchkiss after the battle of McDowell. (LOC)

Jackson was strongly desirous of doing something to disrupt Banks's forward progress, especially if it could help Johnston on the Peninsula. Lincoln had finally decided to approve McDowell's advance to Fredericksburg. On April 21, Gen. Robert E. Lee, assigned by Jefferson Davis as commander of all military operations in Virginia, wrote to Jackson, "I have no doubt that an attempt will be made to occupy Fredericksburg and use it as a base of operations against Richmond. Our present force there is very small and cannot be reinforced except by weakening our corps. If you can use General Ewell's division in an attack on Banks, it will prove a great relief to the pressure on Fredericksburg."

Over the next week, Jackson and Lee corresponded on the best move to make. Lee suggested that if Banks was too strong, Jackson and Ewell should move east and attack the Federals at either Warrenton or Fredericksburg. "The blow, wherever struck, must, to be successful, be sudden and heavy." On April 26, when Banks moved two brigades to Harrisonburg, Jackson directed Ewell to move west from Gordonsville to Stanardsville, 20 miles closer to the Valley.

Jackson still felt his best option was to attack Banks when the opportunity presented itself. He had three plans in mind. If Banks continued his advance on Staunton, he could threaten his flank by leaving Ewell at Swift Run Gap and combining with Allegheny Johnson to attack Frémont. He could also join forces with Ewell, get behind Banks at New Market and induce him to pull back. The third option involved moving east of the Blue Ridge and then north to threaten Winchester. Lee told Jackson the decision was his to make.

Jackson learned that, while Banks remained at Harrisonburg, "a considerable force, under the command of General Milroy, was moving toward Staunton." He decided that in order to prevent Allegheny Johnson from getting caught between Banks and Milroy, he would attempt to outpace the Union forces and join with Johnson to defeat Milroy, and then combine with Ewell to defeat Banks. His maneuvers over the next week baffled friend and foe alike.

On the morning of April 30 Jackson set his army in motion to the south, in the direction of Port Republic. Over the next three days, down muddy roads, in a driving rain, they continued southeast. Jackson's men believed they were actually going further east to join Johnston near Richmond, and even Ewell, who had moved into Jackson's former camps at Swift Run Gap to keep an eye on Banks, was kept in the dark.

When the sun finally returned on May 3, Jackson's army had crossed the Blue Ridge at Brown's Gap and descended on the Virginia Central Railroad station at Mechum River. Now the question was, would the army head east or west? Late on the afternoon of May 4, much to the relief of the citizens of Staunton as well as Allegheny Johnson, Jackson and his staff rode into town. The guessing was over.

Banks, blissfully unaware that Jackson had joined forces with Johnson and interposed himself between Banks and any

"I believe Jackson's movement to be a feint for the relief of Johnson. He cannot move from Port Republic toward my advanced position without leaving Banks in his rear." Milroy to Frémont, May 6, 1862. (LOC)

possible junction with Frémont, continued to ponder his next move. If the disposition of forces was working in Jackson's favor, the numbers were not. Banks still had 19,000 men at his disposal, while Milroy, operating near the town of McDowell, had another 3,000. Frémont's other brigade commander, Robert C. Schenck, was within a day's march of Milroy with 3,000 men, and Frémont himself would soon depart Wheeling, Virginia, bringing the total Union force to over 30,000.

Jackson had approximately 8,000 of his own men and 3,000 of Johnson's to work with. Even with Ewell's 8,000, sitting on Banks's flank at Swift Run Gap, he was heavily outnumbered. Jackson's advantage was in speed and surprise, which he had used to get to Staunton, and now he was about to demonstrate his favorite tactic – that of maneuvering his smaller army in such a way as to find the enemy's weakest spot and overwhelm him.

THE BATTLE OF MCDOWELL, MAY 8

At dawn on May 7 the combined forces of Jackson and Johnson headed west out of Staunton with Johnson in the lead. Joining them, to get some experience in a real campaign, though they wouldn't participate in the battle, were the cadets from the Virginia Military Institute. In their polished uniforms and parade-ground formation they marched in stark contrast to the ragged, gaunt, but just as eager, men of the Valley army.

That afternoon Johnson encountered Milroy's pickets at Rodgers's Tollgate, at the foot of Shenandoah Mountain, 13 miles from McDowell. Milroy had been advised "by my scouts and spies" that the two Confederate generals had combined their forces and were advancing on him. Expecting Schenck to soon reinforce him, Milroy ordered his entire command to fall back and concentrate at McDowell. That night, Johnson went into camp at Shaw's Fork 6 miles to the east, with Jackson 10 miles away at Buffalo Gap.

Milroy recognized that McDowell was nearly indefensible. The town sat on the shallow Bull Pasture River, surrounded on all sides by high ground, with Bull Pasture Mountain 2 miles to the east across the river. The Parkersburg–Staunton Turnpike, along which Jackson's men were coming, connected McDowell with Staunton. North of the turnpike, running southwest to the riverbank, was Hull's Ridge, with an outcropping known as Cedar Knob at its southern tip. Running south of the turnpike and overlooking the town, was Sitlington's Hill, a mile-long plateau with steep ravines and sharp ridges rising 500ft to its broad, rugged top.

Milroy had his men up and ready before daybreak on May 8. He deployed his infantry along the west bank of the rain-swollen river and his artillery both on Cemetery Hill and near the McDowell Presbyterian Church. The Confederate advance ascended Bull Pasture Mountain where Jackson was able to view the Union forces across the river. With him was Hotchkiss, who he directed to map the entire front, including the disposition of the enemy's forces. Johnson continued to Sitlington Hill.

At 10am, with still no attack from Jackson, Schenck arrived on the scene. "By leaving my baggage train under a guard in my last camp, on the road 14 miles from McDowell, I was able to push forward so as to make the whole distance (34 miles) in twenty-three hours." Schenck brought with him elements of three tired regiments totaling 1,300 infantry, a battery from the 1st Ohio Artillery, and 250 troopers of the Connecticut Cavalry.

Milroy was more than grateful for the support and briefed Schenck, who was now the senior officer on the field. Milroy wanted to launch an immediate attack, hoping to catch the advancing Confederates by surprise before they could get their artillery on the heights. Schenck initially disagreed, but realized that they would be hard pressed to execute a withdrawal from the town without knowing the full disposition of the force against them. "We agreed that the better plan would be to send, that evening, whatever portion of our united forces was available for the attack up the side of the mountain to assault the enemy and deliver a blow, if we could, and then retire from his front before he had recovered from the surprise of such a movement."

Late in the morning, reports of Confederate skirmishers on Bull Pasture Mountain began to come in. Milroy sent a company of the 73rd Ohio Infantry with orders to cross the river and climb Sitlington's Hill in order to reconnoiter the front. He then deployed the 82nd Ohio Infantry, supported

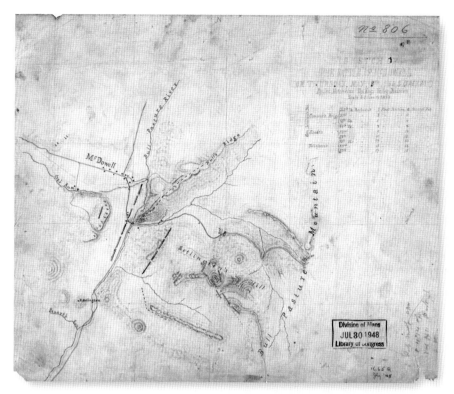

Division of Maps
JUL 30 1948
Library of Congress

"I made him [Jackson] a map of McDowell and vicinity, showing the enemy's position, as in full view before us." Hotchkiss, May 8, 1862. (LOC)

by a battery of the 12th Ohio Artillery, to Cedar Knob. With nothing much to aim at, the gunners began lobbing shells across the road at the desultory rate of about one every five minutes. Just after noon, the artillerymen spotted a company of the enemy's infantry on the crest of Sitlington Hill. What they first took to be skirmishers turned out to be Allegheny Johnson "with a party of 30 men and several officers." The Rebels had arrived.

Johnson's regiments now began to come up. The 52nd Virginia Infantry was posted on the left of the hill, and soon began skirmishing with the 73rd Ohio Infantry. Milroy sent two more companies of the 73rd Ohio Infantry, two companies of the 32nd Ohio Infantry, and a company of the 75th Ohio Infantry across the river as additional skirmishers. Jackson took little notice of the small-scale fighting that was going on around the hill, and discussed with Johnson his plan to try and find an alternate route across the river in order to stage his own attack on Milroy the next day. He tasked Johnson with securing the hill, while he continued to explore ways to get behind Milroy, never expecting the Federal commander to take the offensive.

About 3pm, responding to reports that the Rebels were attempting to place artillery on the hill, Milroy ordered the remaining companies of the 25th and 75th Ohio Infantry that had not previously been involved in the skirmishing, 16 in all, across the river and up the hill. They advanced "up a precipitous mountain side upon an adversary protected by intrenchments and the natural formation of the mountain." They went in with limited support from Milroy's main artillery batteries, 18 guns in all, which remained on the west side of the river. The artillerymen dug deep trenches behind the guns in an attempt to elevate the barrels high enough to reach the top of the hill, but with minimal effect. The 2nd West Virginia Infantry crossed the river and occupied Hull's Hill, north of the pike.

THE BATTLE OF McDOWELL, MAY 8 (pp. 50–51)

On May 8, 1862, near the town of McDowell, Union Brigadier-General Robert Milroy faced the combined forces of Confederate General "Allegheny" Johnson and Stonewall Jackson. Milroy deployed his men on the west side of Bull Pasture River, as Johnson's men filed into position two miles east, across the river, on Sitlington's Hill. Late in the afternoon, believing that the Rebels were placing artillery on the hill, Milroy surprised the Confederate commanders by ordering the 25th and 75th Ohio Infantry regiments to attack.

Jackson remained behind the line, shuffling regiments to Johnson on top of the hill, as the battle increased in intensity. The 12th Georgia formed the center of an arcing, and rapidly expanding, Rebel line.

Colonel Nathaniel C. McLean, commanding the 75th Ohio, reported that, "The side of the mountain up which I was compelled to make the attack was entirely destitute of protection either from trees or rocks, and so steep that the men were at times compelled to march either to one side or the other to make the ascent."

The 25th and 75th Ohio (1) attacked the 12th Georgia and the left companies of the 44th Virginia (2). The Georgians bore the brunt of the attack. Their commander had placed them on a spur of Sitlington's Hill, in a salient from the main Confederate line. They were exposed on three sides to the Union advance, and had to stand up to fire their smoothbore muskets down on the assaulting Federals. With the late afternoon sun in their faces, the Georgians were silhouetted against the sky for the Union troops, who tended to remain in the shadows as they clambered up the steep hillside. Additionally, the Confederates tended to fire too high because of the slope of the hill. The 12th Georgia suffered the highest casualty rate of any unit involved in the battle, accounting for over 35 percent of the total Confederate casualties reported.

At about 4pm Milroy sent in the 82nd Ohio Infantry of Schenck's Brigade, and the rest of the 32nd Ohio Infantry along with the 3rd West Virginia Infantry of his own, "to turn the right flank of the enemy, and if possible, attack them in the rear." The approach to the top was through a ravine on the north side of the hill just off the road. As these men were advancing up the pike, he directed a 6-pdr cannon, which had to be hauled by hand, to Hull's Hill to fire on the Confederate right. As the 3rd West Virginia Infantry advanced along the pike, the two remaining regiments of Johnson's Brigade, the 25th and 31st Virginia Infantry, were posted in an elevated piece of wood to the right of the main Confederate line. When the 31st was ordered to join the rest of its brigade on the hill, about 5pm, the 21st Virginia took its place. Jackson reported that "the fire was now rapid and well sustained on both sides and the conflict fierce and sanguinary."

At the top of the hill the 12th Georgia Infantry formed the center of the Rebel line, with the 48th Virginia Infantry on the left supporting the previously deployed 52nd, and the 44th Virginia Infantry on the right near the ravine. The 32nd and 82nd Ohio Infantry met the 25th Virginia Infantry and the right companies of the 44th Virginia Infantry, while the 25th and 75th Ohio Infantry attacked the 12th Georgia Infantry and the left companies of the 44th Virginia Infantry. The fiercest fighting raged from 4.30 to about 8.30pm, and focused on the 12th Georgia Infantry. Jackson ordered the 23rd and 37th Virginia Infantry of Taliaferro's Brigade into the fray and they were advanced to the center of the line held by the Georgians. Every attempt by the five Union regiments engaged, nearly 2,500 men in all, to penetrate the center or turn the Confederate right flank was repulsed. Jackson had declined to send artillery up the hill because of his concern that the rugged terrain would prevent him from saving it should the Confederate position be overrun, making this almost entirely an infantry battle by both sides.

As darkness descended on the field, the firing began to slacken off. Some men attempted to fire at the muzzle flashes of their opponents, but with ammunition running out the fight was over. Union forces withdrew back across the river carrying their wounded with them. Schenck reported 256 total casualties, including 26 killed, from the five Union regiments that had been employed. Johnson and the six regiments of his Army of the Northwest, about 2,800 men in all, supported by three of Jackson's regiments with their 1,400 men, suffered 498 casualties, including 54 officers. Among the wounded, was Allegheny Johnson himself, who had been shot in the ankle and had to retire from the field.

At 2am on the 9th Schenck and Milroy ordered a general withdrawal towards Franklin, 32 miles to the northwest. When Jackson rode out at dawn, the 73rd Ohio Infantry, acting as a rearguard for the retreating Federals, was just departing McDowell. "God blessed our arms with victory at M'Dowell yesterday," Jackson reported. It was certainly a mixed victory. The Federals had seized the initiative, battling uphill against superior numbers, and inflicted nearly double the number of casualties on the enemy as they themselves suffered. More importantly, after the battle, they had been able to get away virtually unscathed. But it was still a victory in the eyes of the Southern people and relieved the threat to Staunton from the west. More importantly, it demonstrated Jackson's ability to maneuver his strategically smaller force when compared to the numbers Banks and Frémont could potentially bring against him, and achieve tactical superiority at the point of attack.

For the next three days Jackson's men kept up the pursuit. The Federal rearguard harassed them every step of the way. At one point, the forests along the road were set on fire, sending up columns of smoke that hid Federal riflemen from view and enabled them to fire on their Rebel pursuers. On May 12 the Federal columns arrived in Franklin and, with Frémont close at hand, Jackson made the decision to give up the chase and return to the Valley.

AFTER MCDOWELL, MAY 9–22

On May 13, Ewell, who had been fidgeting at Swift Run Gap for a week, received the message that Jackson was on his way back to the Valley. Jackson directed him to pursue Banks if the Federal commander withdrew from Strasburg. Ewell would have been only too happy to comply with that directive if he hadn't received conflicting orders from Johnston, who was under intense pressure to defend Richmond in the face of McClellan's advance. The Confederate authorities were considering abandoning the capital and Johnston told Ewell that if Banks moved eastward to join McDowell at Fredericksburg, then Ewell should immediately leave the Valley and return to Richmond. When Ewell learned that Shields's Division had crossed the Blue Ridge heading east he was in a quandary over whose orders he should follow.

As Jackson was marching towards Harrisonburg and Ewell was fretting in the Luray Valley, Banks was consolidating his headquarters at Strasburg. He put his men to work building entrenchments, and, even though he was convinced that Jackson posed no immediate threat, he was becoming sensitive to the fact that his army was rapidly being depleted. Shields had been ordered to Fredericksburg on May 12, effectively cutting Banks's force in half, and four days later Banks was tasked to provide two regiments to guard the railroad between Strasburg and Front Royal. He complied, while responding that this would significantly reduce his force "which is already too small to defend Strasburg, if attacked."

Banks arrived in Strasburg and began building entrenchments, similar to those pictured here, to stave off Jackson's presumed attack from the south. The entrenchments left the north side of town open. (LOC)

McDowell, Front Royal, and Winchester, March to May 1862

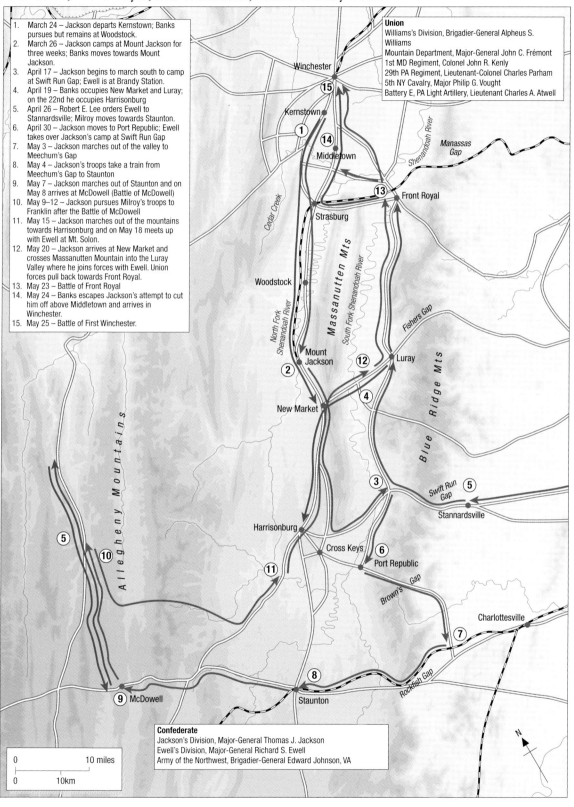

1. March 24 – Jackson departs Kernstown; Banks pursues but remains at Woodstock.
2. March 26 – Jackson camps at Mount Jackson for three weeks; Banks moves towards Mount Jackson.
3. April 17 – Jackson begins to march south to camp at Swift Run Gap; Ewell is at Brandy Station.
4. April 19 – Banks occupies New Market and Luray; on the 22nd he occupies Harrisonburg.
5. April 26 – Robert E. Lee orders Ewell to Stannardsville; Milroy moves towards Staunton.
6. April 30 – Jackson moves to Port Republic; Ewell takes over Jackson's camp at Swift Run Gap
7. May 3 – Jackson marches out of the valley to Meechum's Gap.
8. May 4 – Jackson's troops take a train from Meechum's Gap to Staunton.
9. May 7 – Jackson marches out of Staunton and on May 8 arrives at McDowell (Battle of McDowell)
10. May 9–12 – Jackson pursues Milroy's troops to Franklin after the Battle of McDowell
11. May 15 – Jackson marches out of the mountains towards Harrisonburg and on May 18 meets up with Ewell at Mt. Solon.
12. May 20 – Jackson arrives at New Market and crosses Massanutten Mountain into the Luray Valley where he joins forces with Ewell. Union forces pull back towards Front Royal.
13. May 23 – Battle of Front Royal
14. May 24 – Banks escapes Jackson's attempt to cut him off above Middletown and arrives in Winchester.
15. May 25 – Battle of First Winchester.

Union
Williams's Division, Brigadier-General Alpheus S. Williams
Mountain Department, Major-General John C. Frémont
1st MD Regiment, Colonel John R. Kenly
29th PA Regiment, Lieutenant-Colonel Charles Parham
5th NY Cavalry, Major Philip G. Vought
Battery E, PA Light Artillery, Lieutenant Charles A. Atwell

Confederate
Jackson's Division, Major-General Thomas J. Jackson
Ewell's Division, Major-General Richard S. Ewell
Army of the Northwest, Brigadier-General Edward Johnson, VA

0   10 miles
0   10km

On May 17 Ewell felt compelled to ride to Mount Solon, midway between Staunton and Harrisonburg, to confer with Jackson. Lee had now entered the fray and, as Jefferson Davis's chief military advisor, he believed that the best way to disrupt the Federal Army's drive on Richmond was to threaten an attack by Jackson on Washington. Lee wrote to Jackson: "Whatever movement you make against Banks, do it speedily, and if successful drive him back towards the Potomac, and create the impression, as far as possible, that you design threatening that line." Johnston believed that Banks was too well protected by his fortified entrenchments at Strasburg, and that an attack there was too risky. Johnston wanted Ewell to march to Richmond. Jackson believed that Ewell had been detached to him and wanted him to march on Luray. Ewell needed a decision, and Jackson telegraphed Lee asking for direction. Lee responded two days later. Ewell would stay with Jackson.

Up until then, Banks had been reporting "no indications of infantry in the Valley," despite some minor brushes with Ashby's cavalry. With Shields's departure, his available strength stood at 4,476 infantry, 1,600 cavalry, and 16 artillery pieces consisting of ten Parrott guns and six smoothbores. He could also count an additional 2,500 infantry, six companies of cavalry, and six artillery pieces on the Manassas Gap Railroad between Strasburg and Manassas. On May 20 he became aware for the first time that Jackson had not only returned from Shenandoah Mountain but was within 8 miles of Harrisonburg. He was certain that Ewell was still at Swift Run Gap and estimated the combined forces of Jackson and Ewell at about 16,000.

Banks was right about the numbers, but dangerously wrong on the locations of the two Confederate commanders. Jackson's Division, consisting of the First, Second, and Third Brigades which had accompanied him to McDowell, supported by Ashby's 7th Virginia Cavalry, and five batteries of artillery manning 22 guns, arrived at New Market on the 20th. Ewell's Division, consisting of the brigades of Brigadier-Generals Richard Taylor, Isaac Trimble, Arnold Elzey, and Colonel W. C. Scott, as well as the independent 1st Maryland Infantry, Brig. Gen. G. H. Steuart's Cavalry, and six batteries of artillery numbering 26 guns, was at Luray.

Ewell's men were new to Jackson. Taylor was the son of former President Zachary Taylor and brother-in-law to Jefferson Davis. His brigade consisted of four Louisiana regiments and Maj. Chatham Roberdeau Wheat's "Louisiana Tiger" Battalion. Trimble was a Virginian with a brigade made up of Alabama, Georgia, Mississippi, and North Carolina regiments. Elzey, from Maryland, commanded one Georgia and three Virginia regiments. Scott had been the commander of the 44th Virginia Infantry and took over the Second Brigade when Steuart took command of the cavalry. Taylor and Elzey had both been at Manassas, and so had battle experience, and Scott had been part of Allegheny Johnson's command at McDowell. Trimble, however, was an engineer, having previously been responsible for battery construction along the Potomac and around Norfolk, Virginia. His inexperience would not turn out to be a problem.

On the 21st Jackson's men, expecting to continue marching north towards Strasburg, suddenly turned east and crossed into the Luray Valley. As he had on the march to McDowell, Jackson kept his plans to himself, but this time his men trusted that the "Mighty Stonewall" knew what he was doing. They joined up with Ewell on the other side of Massanutten Mountain, and, by the evening of the 22nd, Ewell's lead brigade, Taylor's Louisianans, went into camp 10 miles south of Front Royal.

Jackson again surprised his own men by crossing the 2,700ft Massanutten Mountain on May 21 to join Ewell for the attack on Front Royal, thereby flanking Banks at Strasburg. (LOC)

If Jackson's troops were uncertain of their commander's ultimate objective, Banks was totally in the dark. With the combined divisions of Jackson and Ewell on the eastern side of Massanutten Mountain, only 15 miles away, Banks was reporting that: "I do not wish to excite alarm unnecessarily – I am compelled to believe that he (Jackson) meditates attack here. I regard it as certain that he will move north as far as New Market." The Federal leadership in Washington had no idea that Jackson had even left Harrisonburg, let alone joined forces with Ewell. They were preparing to participate in a Grand Review of McDowell's Corps, which was scheduled to depart Fredericksburg for the Peninsula on March 26. Ashby's presence in front of Strasburg continued to impress Banks with the idea that Jackson would soon be marching down the Valley Pike.

THE BATTLE OF FRONT ROYAL, MAY 23

What Front Royal may have lacked in size it made up for in strategic location, situated as it was at the confluence of the North and South Forks of the Shenandoah, with roads running to Winchester and Strasburg, and served by the Manassas Gap Railroad. As Jackson approached on the morning of May 23 his plan was to capture or disperse the Union garrison there "and get in the rear of Banks or compel him to abandon his fortifications at Strasburg."

At about 10am he halted near Asbury Chapel, 4 miles south of town. There he learned of a side road that paralleled the Luray and Front Royal Turnpike, which would skirt the Federal picket line and provide good ground for deployment. He ordered Col. Bradley T. Johnson and the 1st Maryland Infantry to lead the advance and sent Turner Ashby, with his 7th Cavalry and accompanied by Lt. Col. Thomas Flournoy with the 6th Virginia Cavalry, northwest across the Shenandoah River to Buckton Station on the Manassas Gap Railroad to cut communications between Front Royal and Strasburg.

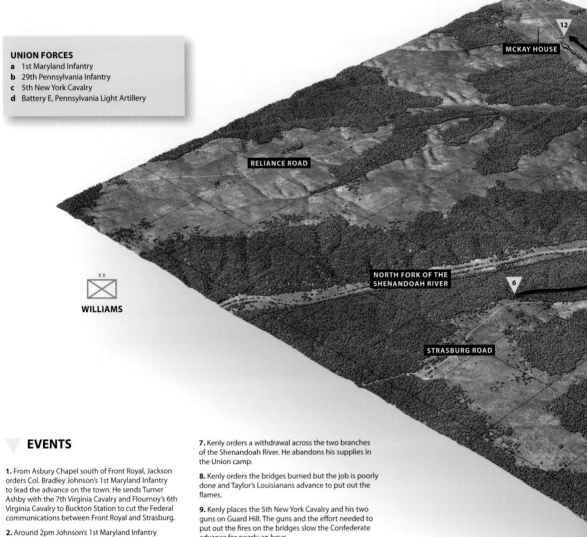

UNION FORCES
- **a** 1st Maryland Infantry
- **b** 29th Pennsylvania Infantry
- **c** 5th New York Cavalry
- **d** Battery E, Pennsylvania Light Artillery

MCKAY HOUSE

RELIANCE ROAD

NORTH FORK OF THE SHENANDOAH RIVER

STRASBURG ROAD

XX
WILLIAMS

▼ **EVENTS**

1. From Asbury Chapel south of Front Royal, Jackson orders Col. Bradley Johnson's 1st Maryland Infantry to lead the advance on the town. He sends Turner Ashby with the 7th Virginia Cavalry and Flournoy's 6th Virginia Cavalry to Buckton Station to cut the Federal communications between Front Royal and Strasburg.

2. Around 2pm Johnson's 1st Maryland Infantry encounters pickets from Col. John R. Kenly's 1st Maryland Infantry south of Front Royal. Kenly pulls his men back through town to Richardson's Hill.

3. Johnson, followed by Wheat's 6th Louisiana Infantry, comes under fire from Kenly's guns on the hill.

4. Hearing the sound of the guns, Major Philip Vought arrives from Strasburg with 100 men of the 5th New York Cavalry and leads a cavalry charge but realizes the Confederate forces are too large and instead he looks for Kenly on the hill.

5. After two hours of fighting Johnson directs the 6th Louisiana Infantry through woods west of the road toward the Union camp to flank the Union position.

6. At the same time Flournoy is spotted returning to Front Royal after his attack on Buckton Station.

7. Kenly orders a withdrawal across the two branches of the Shenandoah River. He abandons his supplies in the Union camp.

8. Kenly orders the bridges burned but the job is poorly done and Taylor's Louisianans advance to put out the flames.

9. Kenly places the 5th New York Cavalry and his two guns on Guard Hill. The guns and the effort needed to put out the fires on the bridges slow the Confederate advance for nearly an hour.

10. Around 6pm Kenly sees Flournoy's cavalry fording the river and orders a further withdrawal up the Winchester Turnpike to the vicinity of Fairview to make a last stand. He orders the artillery to halt and prepare to fire while directing the New York Cavalry to counter-charge the enemy. Neither of these orders is accomplished.

11. The 6th Louisiana Infantry crosses the bridge and advances towards Kenly's position.

12. As Kenly realizes that the artillery has continued to flee to the north, Vought's 5th New York Cavalry suddenly rushes back in disarray through the Union troops, hotly pursued by the 6th Virginia Cavalry. Kenly is struck down and captured along with the majority of his men.

THE BATTLE OF FRONT ROYAL, MAY 23, 1862
Ewell's Division attacks Kenly's 1st Maryland Regiment

CONFEDERATE FORCES
Ewell's Division
Second Brigade – Col. W. C. Scott
2 1st Maryland Infantry
Eighth Brigade – Brig. Gen. Richard Taylor
1 6th Louisiana Infantry
3 Wheat's Battalion
Cavalry Brigade – Col. Thomas T. Munford
4 6th Virginia Cavalry

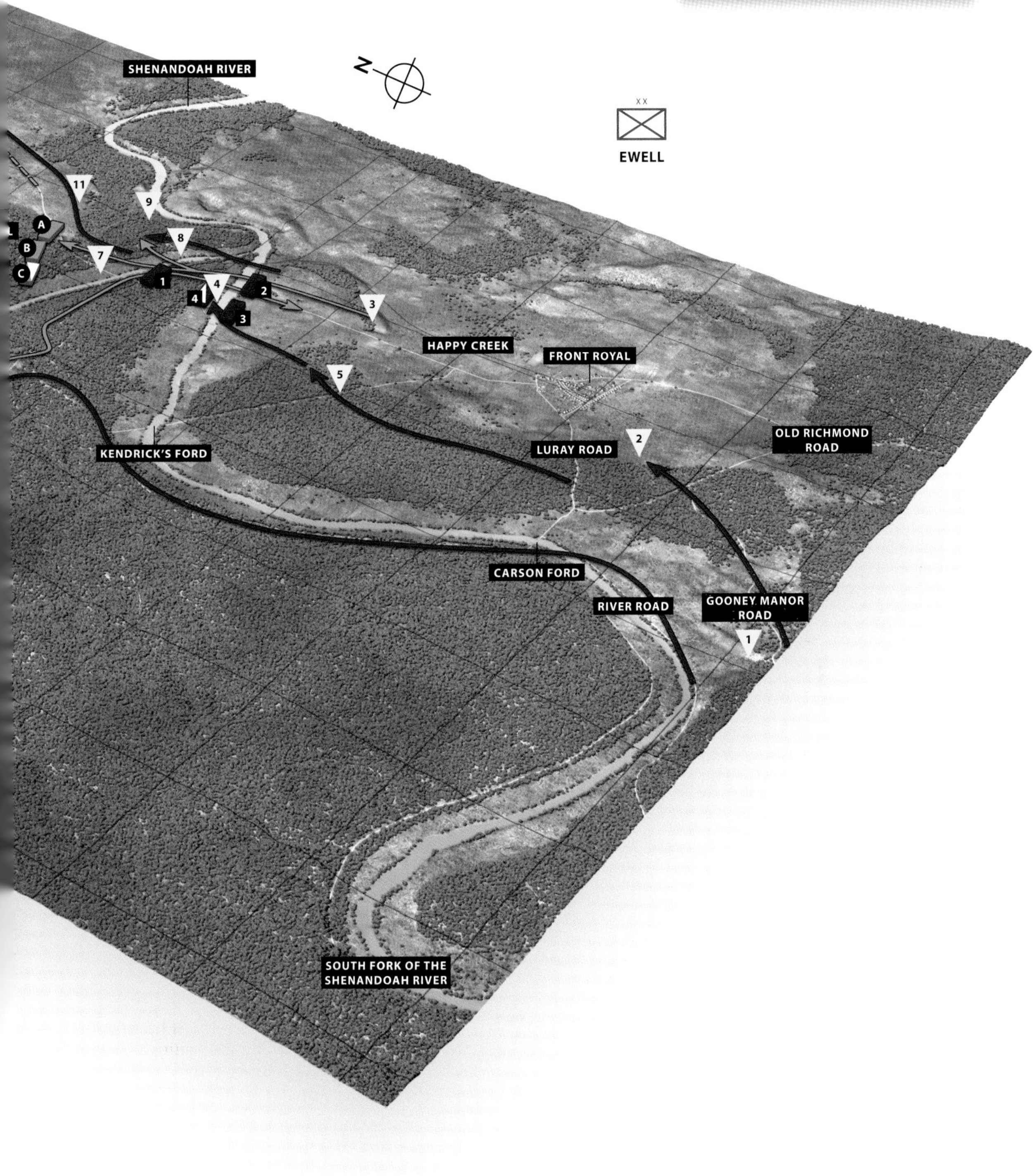

SHENANDOAH RIVER

EWELL

HAPPY CREEK

FRONT ROYAL

KENDRICK'S FORD

LURAY ROAD

OLD RICHMOND ROAD

CARSON FORD

RIVER ROAD

GOONEY MANOR ROAD

SOUTH FORK OF THE SHENANDOAH RIVER

59

In May 1862 Front Royal was a community of approximately 600 inhabitants, strategically located at the northern end of the Luray Valley. Banks provided a small garrison there to guard the railroad and a Federal supply depot. (LOC)

In one of the many strange quirks of the war, the Federal forces in the town consisted of the Union Army's 1st Maryland Infantry under the command of Col. John R. Kenly. To face the 17,000-man Rebel onslaught, Kenly had nine companies totaling 775 men available for duty, along with scattered elements of the 29th Pennsylvania Infantry who were assigned to guard the railroad in the vicinity of Front Royal, and two 10-pdr Parrott guns. Kenly would be augmented by a detachment of the 5th New York Cavalry, which arrived from Strasburg about an hour after the battle started, "making in all 1,063 men." Kenly's pickets were posted on the southwest side of town, crossing the pike and running to the Gooney Manor Road, the side road Jackson was now following.

Just before 2pm the Marylanders of Johnson's regiment overran the Marylanders of Kenly's picket line about a mile and a half south of town. Kenly had directed his men to fall back on the main Federal camp north of town in the event of an attack. Although several were captured, the majority escaped to spread the alarm, and Kenly immediately deployed his regiment to confront the enemy. He realized very quickly that he was up against a large force.

Kenly placed his two rifled guns on the 150ft Richardson's Hill half a mile east of his camp, between the rail line and the main road leading from the town. Johnson's Marylanders, followed closely by Wheat's Battalion, with the 6th Louisiana supporting them, came under their well-directed fire as they emerged from the town around 2.30pm. The first Confederate guns to come up were smoothbore cannons, which were placed on Prospect Hill one and three-quarters miles to the south. They were completely ineffectual, not having the range of the Union's Parrotts, and had to be re-hitched to their carriages and moved forward. Considering the small force at his command, Kenly put up a stiff resistance and the Confederate advance was stalled.

Wheat's Louisiana Tigers joined Johnson's men behind a stone wall below Richardson's Hill. As the Rebels were getting into position, Major Philip G. Vought arrived from Strasburg with about 100 men of the 5th New York Cavalry. Riding to the sound of the guns, with little awareness of the overall situation, he initially "charged with my cavalry down the hill, intending to charge across the plain, being supported by the artillery." Realizing that the enemy force in his front was larger than he had anticipated, he immediately turned about and sought out Kenly, who placed him in line in rear of the artillery.

For nearly two hours the Federal troops held off the assault. About 4pm as as the fighting raged at the hill, Johnson directed the 6th Louisiana Infantry to flank the Union position through some woods west of the road toward the Union camp. Colonel Stapleton Crutchfield, Jackson's Chief of Artillery, finally managed to bring up his rifled guns to counter the Union battery. About 4.30pm a messenger notified Kenly that the Confederate cavalry was advancing from the west between the two river branches in his rear. It was Flournoy returning from his attack on Buckton Station. The Union position had been flanked.

Kenly ordered a withdrawal to a new position across the two branches of the river. The Front Royal Turnpike Bridge and the Manassas Gap Railroad Bridge crossed the south fork of the Shenandoah a half mile north of Richardson's Hill. The railroad turned west between the two branches of the river, while the road continued north across a second bridge over the north fork. Kenly had previously ordered the camp equipment to be loaded onto his wagons, but it was now evident that the supplies could not be saved and he ordered everything to be burned. "It was painfully apparent that I was being surrounded."

Kenly ordered the bridges to be burned behind the retreating Federals. This was "inefficiently done," and Taylor's Louisianans charged into the flames to fight the fire. Kenly now placed the New York cavalry and his two guns on Guard Hill, a point of high ground across the north fork, to harass the pursuing Rebels. Their continued stubborn resistance, coupled with the fact that the "heat from the fire on the nearest bridge must have prevented it from being crossed for a considerable length of time," slowed the Confederate advance for nearly another hour. Kenly rode forward to personally assess the destruction of the bridges when he discovered that "the river below the bridges was alive with horsemen, crossing in two different places by fording." Flournoy's cavalry was swimming across the river.

It was now nearly 6pm and Kenly ordered a further withdrawal up the Winchester Turnpike to the crossroad leading to Middletown to "make a last stand." Leaving Vought's cavalry to guard their retreat, the Federal infantry and artillery managed to get nearly 4 miles from the river. With barely an hour of daylight remaining Kenly "commenced to indulge a hope that I might yet save my command, when the sudden appearance of cavalry galloping through the fields on my left satisfied me that I was lost."

As if to confirm the obvious, Maj. Vought rode up to tell Kenly that he could no longer hold back the attack on his front. Johnson's 1st Maryland Infantry and Wheat's Tigers may not have been able to pass up the potential bounty left in the smoldering Yankee camp, but the 6th Louisiana Infantry had continued on and finally made its way across the bridges.

"I discovered that the river below the bridges was alive with horsemen, crossing in two different places by fording." The photo shows the site of the old bridge where Flournoy's men crossed. (Author's collection)

Kenly attempted to deploy his men in the field off the road, while ordering the artillery to halt and the New York cavalry to countercharge. When he realized that his artillery was still retreating he "dashed forward to learn why my orders had not been obeyed, when the discharge of firearms and the rush of cavalry caused me to turn in time to see that the cavalry had not charged the enemy, but were running over my men, who had not yet left the road, and were closely followed by the enemy's horse."

Kenly's infantrymen unleashed a volley that unhorsed 23 of the 38 troopers of the 6th Virginia Cavalry that were bearing down on them, but they were soon surrounded. Colonel Kenly was struck down by a saber blow to the back of the head, fighting to the last. Initially reported as killed, he survived and was captured along with 690 other members of the garrison; an additional 82 were killed or wounded. Jackson reported 36 casualties out of the more than 3,000 men of his command that participated in the fight, but was able to capture the two Union Parrott guns, which were eventually discovered 4 miles south of Winchester, and "a very large amount of quartermaster and commissary stores." Most importantly, "the enemy's flank was turned and the road was opened to Winchester."

THE FIRST BATTLE OF WINCHESTER, MAY 25

Banks received word of the attack on Front Royal around 4pm on the 23rd from a trooper of the 5th New York Cavalry who Kenly had dispatched as he was organizing his defense on Richardson's Hill. He was still considering just what the information meant when, around 5.30pm, a messenger arrived from Lt. Col. Charles Parham, commander of the 29th Pennsylvania Infantry, confirming the trooper's report. Banks ordered the 3rd Wisconsin Infantry to Kenly's assistance, but hesitated sending additional reinforcements without having a better picture of the overall situation. He sent word of the attack to Secretary of War Stanton, estimating the enemy force at Front Royal at around 5,000 men, and requested reinforcements if any were available.

Survivors from Front Royal began straggling in with ever-worsening tales of the disaster. By 10pm Banks had heard enough to convince him that, if Ewell was on his flank in force, he needed to consider moving his supply train to Winchester and recall the scattered elements of his command. At midnight, a message arrived from Maj. Vought, the 5th New York Cavalry commander who had managed to escape to Winchester, confirming Kenly's surrender and the loss of Front Royal. The picture was getting bleaker by the minute. Ewell was somewhere between him and Winchester, while Jackson must be approaching from the south. He directed his staff to prepare to evacuate Strasburg.

At daybreak on the 24th Banks reported to Stanton that the Confederate attack on Front Royal was "probably Ewell's force, passing through Shenandoah Valley. Jackson is still in our front." Believing that the greatest danger to his march was from the south, Banks ordered the wagon train to the front of the column, followed by the infantry. They were organized with Col. Dudley Donnelly's First Brigade in the lead, Col. George Gordon's Third Brigade, less the 3rd Wisconsin Infantry, in the center, and Brig. Gen. John Hatch's cavalry command (5th New York, 1st Vermont, 1st Maine, 1st Maryland, a battery of the Pennsylvania Light Artillery, and one howitzer from the 4th US Artillery) as the rearguard. Hatch's men were given the responsibility of burning any supplies left behind.

Finally, he sent the remaining companies of the 29th Pennsylvania Infantry, supported by elements of the 1st Michigan Cavalry, to reconnoiter along Chapel Road, a country lane which connected Middletown, four miles north, with Cedarville on the Front Royal–Winchester Road. They advanced several miles and, seeing nothing of significance to report, turned back. In one of the smartest moves he made all day, Banks, feeling cautious, decided to send the 1st Maine Cavalry under Lt. Col. Calvin S. Douty back down the Chapel Road to see if they could find the enemy. Feeling he had covered his options as best he could, Banks ordered the 500-wagon train forward at 9am for the 20-mile trek to Winchester.

"It was now nearly 6 o'clock, and determined to make a last stand at the cross-road leading to Middletown I hurried on to gain this point." Kenly was surrounded by the 6th Virginia Cavalry near this house, known as Fairview. (Author's collection)

Confederate soldiers couldn't pass up "Commissary" Banks's wagon train. "Lemons, oranges, dates, hermetically sealed fruits and vegetables, candies, jellies, pickles, tea, coffee, sugars, etc," remarked one infantryman. (LOC)

Jackson and Ewell had spent the night of the 23rd with the lead elements of the army at Cedarville, the site of Kenly's surrender 4 miles north of Front Royal. They set out on the Winchester Road around 6am. Jackson dispatched Brig. Gen. Steuart, temporarily in command of the 2nd and 6th Virginia Cavalry, cross-country to Newtown on the Valley Pike between Middletown and Winchester "to observe the movements of the enemy at that point." Two hours later, the head of the column reached Nineveh, 6 miles north, and Jackson called a halt for breakfast with Ewell; the rest of the army was strung out a considerable distance behind them.

Steuart arrived in Newtown to find the road crowded with wagons heading north. This was the lead portion of Banks's train, containing the sick and wounded from Strasburg. Steuart charged the wagons and ambulances, capturing about 70 prisoners, and spreading panic up and down the line. He sent word of the column back to Jackson, and then turned south towards Middletown, wreaking havoc along the way.

About this time Trimble was drawing Jackson's attention to a column of smoke coming from the direction of Strasburg. Believing his best chance of intercepting a retreating Banks was at Middletown, 6½ miles to the west on the Valley Pike, Jackson decided to retrace his route to Cedarville. Ewell, with Trimble's Brigade, the 1st Maryland Infantry, and supporting artillery, remained at Nineveh to await instructions. Ashby was to advance toward Middletown with skirmishers from Taylor's Brigade, followed by the rest of the army. None of the roads were particularly good, made worse by a morning rain shower, and none of the Confederate columns knew what to expect to their front.

Banks was approaching Cedar Creek, 2 miles south of Middletown, when he received word of Steuart's attack. Realizing the greater danger was not behind but ahead of him, he ordered Donnelly and the infantry to the front. At Middletown, they found the teamsters attempting to regain control of their wagons, many of which had been abandoned by their drivers in the wake of Steuart's dash south. Steuart's cavalry appeared ahead of them to the east of the road. Donnelly deployed the 46th Pennsylvania Infantry in the

woods to the right of the turnpike with a section of artillery in support. The guns opened up and the 28th New York Infantry drove the Rebel cavalrymen back more than 2 miles from the pike, giving Banks a little breathing space.

As Jackson turned off the Winchester–Front Royal Road at Cedarville, he sent Maj. Hotchkiss with a small cavalry detachment out ahead of the troops while Ashby probed further to the south toward Strasburg. A mile and a half west, Hotchkiss ran into Col. Douty who had been working his way along the Chapel Road with five companies of his own regiment and Collins's squadron of the 1st Vermont Cavalry. According to Douty, "Shots were exchanged, and the enemy fell back." It was now nearly noon.

Hotchkiss rode back to Jackson with the news. Jackson sent him forward again with three companies of the 8th Louisiana Infantry in support. Douty threw out skirmishers to the right and left and sent a courier back to the signal officer posted along the Valley Pike at Middletown to alert Banks. Not knowing the size of Douty's force, Hotchkiss and the Louisianans advanced at a snail's pace and Douty forced the Rebels to work for every inch. He executed a steady and deliberate withdrawal the 4 miles back to Middletown, causing enough uncertainty in Jackson's mind that it delayed the advance by nearly two hours.

At 2.30pm Douty turned off the Chapel Road and back onto the Valley Pike. He learned from the signal officer that Banks and Williams had already passed with the train and infantry. Brigadier-General Hatch, who had been left behind to organize the rearguard, was expected at any moment. Douty led his men into the village of Middletown, south of the crossroads, to wait for Hatch.

The 8th Louisiana Infantry now appeared north of town and the accompanying guns of Chew's Battery began to throw artillery rounds at Douty's men. Douty was about to call for a withdrawal back to Strasburg when Hatch arrived. He deployed Douty and Collins into the side streets and fields east of the turnpike. Ashby now appeared from the woods behind them. The men of the 8th Louisiana Infantry formed in line behind a stone wall north of the town. Hatch gave the command to charge to the men of Douty's 1st Maine Cavalry, and they did, into a wall of fire from the Louisianans.

Captain Collis led his Zouaves down the Valley Pike towards Middletown. This photo shows the direction of his approach and the presumed location of the stone wall at the top of the rise in the background near the white house.
(Author's collection)

THE FIRST BATTLE OF WINCHESTER, MAY 25 (pp. 66–67)

On May 24, 1862, Stonewall Jackson attempted to intercept General Banks's retreat from Strasburg to Winchester. Traveling from Front Royal, where he had forced the surrender of the small Union garrison there the day before, Jackson arrived on the Valley Pike north of Middletown, late in the afternoon. He was just in time to witness a skirmish between the 8th Louisiana and elements of the 1st Michigan and 1st Vermont cavalry, under the command of Brigadier-General Hatch, Banks's cavalry commander. The firefight was brief and the Union troopers were chased off to the west. The evidence of abandoned wagons and horses now led Jackson to believe that Banks's main column had already passed, when he heard gunfire on the south edge of town, leading him to hope that more of Banks's men had been cut off. What he heard was a skirmish precipitated by the appearance of Captain Charles Collis and the Zouaves d'Afrique **(1)**, part of Banks's rearguard. Collis and his men had been about to set fire to the Cedar Creek Bridge two miles to the south when they became aware of the fight going on at Middletown. Leaving the bridge intact, Collis

brought his small contingent down the Pike to investigate. Coming into town, Collis realized that they had been separated from the main column, and quickly formed his men behind a stone wall within 150 paces of the enemy **(2)**. Running toward them was a Confederate Zouave unit, Wheat's Louisiana Tigers **(3)**. "Our first reception was a whole volley of musketry from right to left," Collis reported, "but thanks to our little breastwork, I had but one man injured, and he but slightly." Collis' men returned the fire. Private Harry Handerson was a member of the Louisianans attacking Collis. "A vicious volley of bullets whistled through our disordered ranks, splintering the rails of the neighboring fence and wounding several of my comrades, and looking down the road towards Strasburg, I saw a company of Zouaves firing vigorously upon our advance." The firefight lasted about ten minutes before Collis determined that the Rebels were about to flank his position. He ordered a withdrawal back up the hill, losing three men in the process. They re-crossed the Cedar Creek Bridge, this time burning it in the process.

Jackson arrived in time to watch the one-sided engagement: "In a few moments the turnpike, which had just before teemed with life, presented a most appalling spectacle of carnage and destruction," Douty reported. "The dust was so thick I could neither see nor tell anything in particular, except close by me. I passed over the bodies of men and horses strewn along the road." Falling back through Middletown, Douty escaped with the survivors of the 1st Maine Cavalry west to the Middle Road, where they eventually made their way to Winchester. Hatch and Collins also managed to make their escape. Having not lost a man in his retrograde motion in front of Hotchkiss, Douty reported his losses at Middletown as one man wounded and presumed captured, and 96 missing.

It was now 4pm and Jackson was finally astride the Valley Pike, attempting to determine how much of Banks's wagon train had already passed. Observing the large number of abandoned Federal supply wagons, he dispatched a note to Ewell that read: "The enemy has retreated en masse toward Winchester. Major-General Jackson requests that you will move on Winchester with all the force you have left as promptly as possible." No sooner had the courier departed than Jackson heard gunfire coming from the south. He sent a second note to Ewell telling him to stand put, and requesting he send Elzey's Brigade to Middletown.

The gunfire turned out to be a brief skirmish precipitated by the sudden appearance of a portion of the rearguard left behind by Banks to burn the Cedar Creek Bridge. The firefight, between two units both wearing distinctive Zouave uniforms, was short but distracting enough that Jackson sent the 8th Louisiana Infantry again in pursuit. They had formed a mile and a half-wide line of battle north of the Cedar Creek Bridge when they were finally recalled by Jackson, who had determined that the real prize – the main body of Banks's army – was in the opposite direction.

Jackson's cautious advance from Front Royal, coupled with the skirmishes at Middletown, meant that he had taken far longer than he had anticipated. If he were ever going to catch Banks, he needed to do so without further delay. It was now nearly 6pm and Winchester was still 15 miles away. He penned another message to Ewell directing him to take up the advance. The exchange of notes between Jackson and Ewell had caused the latter to start, then stop, then start again. At 5.45pm, tired of doing nothing, Ewell had written to Jackson suggesting that he march with Trimble's Brigade to Newtown. He waited an hour without reply before deciding to take a chance and proceed anyway, but to Winchester rather than Newtown. Fifteen minutes later, Jackson's note approving his march to Newtown arrived, but by this time Ewell was too far down the road toward Winchester. He decided to continue, and sent the courier back to Jackson, stating so.

So many supplies had been abandoned during Banks's march that the Rebels dubbed him "Commissary Banks." The road was strewn with the debris left in his wake. It was not only the material from the wagons that had been left. The Federal infantrymen had, in many cases, abandoned their knapsacks, much to the delight of their pursuers. Even Ashby's men, along with their commander himself, joined in the plundering.

With Hatch and the rearguard cut off from the rest of the column, the rear of the train was coming under increased harassment as it passed through Newtown. The head of the column was now approaching Kernstown and Banks decided to send back the 2nd Massachusetts Infantry, the 27th Indiana

Infantry, and the 28th New York Infantry "to rescue the rear of the train and hold the enemy in check." A brief artillery duel ensued, forcing the small Rebel force to pull back. The passage of the wagon train continued, although some of the wagons that could not be saved had to be burned. Hatch rejoined the column at this point, after completing an arduous cross-country trek, and continued on to Winchester. It wasn't until 2.00am on the 25th that the 2nd Massachusetts Infantry, the last Federal unit, managed to make their way into town. Around 3am a frustrated Jackson was finally persuaded to stop the advance just north of Kernstown and let his exhausted troops catch a few hours' sleep.

Colonel George Gordon reported on the fight put up by his regiment:

> The Second Massachusetts Regiment made this day a march of 30 miles, nearly 10 miles of which was continued running fight. This noble regiment moved in column along the road, undismayed by an enemy they could not see, firing at the flashes of the rebel rifles, supporting their wounded and carrying their dead. For more than 8 miles they guarded the rear of the column; then with two and a half hours' slumber, uncovered and unprotected, they were aroused by the cannon and musketry that ushered in the battle of Winchester.

Banks notified Stanton of his arrival in Winchester and stated his attention to "return to Strasburg with my command immediately." Stanton replied that the President needed a lot more information on "the force and position of the enemy in your neighborhood," before authorizing any movement from Banks. Estimates of Jackson's and Ewell's combined strength ranged from 15,000 to 30,000 men. With roughly 4,000 Union troops at hand, Banks called his division commanders Williams and Hatch together for a council of war. He was determined to put up some kind of fight. His commanders agreed but with little expectation of success. "That we should all be prisoners of war I had little doubt," Williams stated, "but we could not get away without a show of resistance."

Colonel Donnelly was ordered to occupy the ridges southeast of the town on both sides of the Front Royal Road. Before dawn, he received a verbal order from Banks directing him to "send back the trains of the division towards Martinsburg." The more difficult part of the order directed him to "offer such resistance to the rebels as would develop with more certainty their strength and give time for our transportation wagons to move clear of the route of our retreat." Unfortunately, "the enemy gave us little time to correct our own position or to reconnoiter theirs."

Donnelly's Brigade, numbering 1,700 men, stretched from a hill near the Front Royal Road in a crescent shape around to the southeast. Six guns of the 4th US Artillery and a section of the 1st New York Artillery supported him. Colonel Gordon, with his 2,100-man brigade, occupied the hills nearest the town which commanded the road from Strasburg, and was supported by six 6-pdr Parrotts of Cothran's Battery of the 1st New York Artillery. On the extreme right five companies of the Michigan Cavalry were held in reserve under cover of the hill. Between the two brigades, on an elevation immediately in front of the town, was a section of Captain Robert Hampton's Battery within supporting distance of Hatch's cavalry.

Jackson attacked at first light. Brigadier-General Winder was tasked with seizing the hills occupied by Gordon's Brigade. The 5th Virginia Infantry led

Battery M, 1st NY Light Artillery, with six 10-pdr Parrott guns, similar to those shown here, was posted on Camp Hill southeast of Winchester to support Col. Dudley Donnelly's Brigade. (LOC)

the advance, followed by the 2nd, 4th, 27th, and 33rd Virginia Infantry. About 5.00am they encountered the skirmishers of the 2nd Massachusetts Infantry. Gordon's artillery opened up an enfilading fire on the advancing columns of the Virginians. Jackson placed the two Parrott guns of the Rockbridge Artillery with Captain Joseph Carpenter's and Captain W. E. Cutshaw's batteries on a hill facing the Federal guns, and a two-hour artillery duel went on while the Confederate regiments maneuvered into position.

Just before 7am, Gordon became aware that "large bodies of infantry could be seen making their way in line of battle toward my right." Despite their being somewhat concealed by a ridge and woods in his front, Gordon shifted his regiments in that direction, with the 29th Pennsylvania Infantry and 27th Indiana Infantry moving to the right of the 2nd Massachusetts Infantry, which now became the center, with the 3rd Wisconsin Infantry on the left. He had barely moved his men into position when the full force of the enemy came over the ridge. This was Taylor's Brigade, and it advanced in textbook fashion. "Steadily, and in fine order, mounting the hill, and there fronting the enemy, where he stood in greatest strength, the whole line magnificently swept down the declivity and across the field, driving back the Federal troops and bearing down all opposition before it." Winder's men now joined in the attack, forcing Gordon to give way.

On the Confederate right, Ewell sent in the 21st North Carolina Infantry and 21st Georgia Infantry. Donnelly's 46th Pennsylvania Infantry occupied the west side of the road, the 5th Connecticut Volunteers the east, with Best's Battery of the 4th US Artillery on a hill to the rear. The hills in front were manned by the 10th Maine Infantry, who skirmished briefly with the Rebel pickets before retiring back into town. The 21st North Carolina Infantry emerged from a dense fog that had settled over the field into the waiting guns of Donnelly's men. They fell back, regrouped, and then tried a bayonet charge that was just as severely repulsed. Firing ceased for almost 30 minutes as Ewell moved the 1st Maryland Infantry and Trimble's Brigade to the extreme left of the Union line, threatening to not only outflank it, but also cut off any avenue of retreat.

"I directed the battery to open upon the columns of the enemy evidently moving into position just to the right and front of my center." Colonel George H. Gordon, commanding Banks's right flank at Winchester. (LOC)

Brigadier-General Williams went forward from Banks's headquarters to observe the action on the right. "Before I could reach with all possible speed the crest of the hill upon which Gordon's brigade had moved I saw the artillery were limbering up to move to the rear." He noted members of the 27th Indiana Infantry also falling back despite efforts to rally them, and realized the entire right side of the line was in danger of collapsing. He tried to send the Michigan Cavalry, held in reserve, forward, but they were repulsed as well and he now knew that the only option left was to fall back through the town. He sent a message to Colonel Donnelly directing him to withdraw his brigade by the east side of the town. By 9.30am it was all over.

The retreating Federals passed through Winchester and attempted to regain some form of order as they headed north on the Martinsburg Road. Behind them, the Confederate infantrymen became hopelessly entangled once again in the mass of material left behind by the fleeing Union troops, and in the cheering throngs of citizens who welcomed their liberators. To Jackson, Banks's troops were a disorganized mass, defenseless and scattered and he searched desperately for his cavalry to take up the chase as his infantry and artillery were exhausted from the battle, while the distance between them and the enemy was increasing by the minute.

Steuart was still supporting Ewell on the east side of the town. When Jackson did manage to locate him and ordered him to chase down the retreating Federals, Steuart claimed that only Ewell could task him. "Never have I seen an opportunity when it was in the power of cavalry to reap a richer harvest of the fruits of victory," Jackson noted. Steuart did take up the pursuit about an hour later and succeeded in capturing a number of prisoners, but it was much too late. Ashby eventually joined Steuart just south of Bunker Hill, nearly 10 miles away, but Banks's infantry held them off. They followed as far as Martinsburg before turning back. Ashby reported that he had been on the east side of Winchester attempting to cut off the enemy's line of retreat in that direction. Jackson could only ponder what might have been.

The Federals withdrew in three columns with Gordon on the turnpike, Donnelly to the east guarding the right flank, and a vast array of stragglers in between. Banks moved back and forth through the columns rallying the troops and keeping them moving forward. The survivors reached Martinsburg at 1.30pm in remarkably good order considering that they'd been routed, and Banks called a halt until 5.00pm. They then pushed on to the Williamsport crossing on the Potomac where they went into makeshift camps before midnight, completing a march of 35 miles from Winchester, and over 60 miles in two days. The crossing into Maryland began at 2am the following morning.

CROSS KEYS AND PORT REPUBLIC, JUNE 8 AND 9

Newspaper accounts of Banks's defeat were as varied in their opinions of what it all meant as were the reports of the commanders involved. The *Richmond Examiner* announced that "Richmond yesterday experienced a decided and wholesome feeling of elation and rejoicing," while the *New York Times* correspondent in Washington reported: "We have passed a very exciting day in Washington. The secession sympathizers too greatly elated to conceal their joy, openly expressing their belief that the hosts of Jeff Davis will overrun Maryland and the District within twenty-four hours." A subsequent *New York Times* article was more measured: "It certainly is not easy to see from what quarter Washington can be deemed to be in danger just now. Jackson is the only force that seems to be marching *toward* the Capital from any quarter." The reporter concluded, "Washington is about as safe as Boston."

Whatever the public believed, Jackson's sudden advance could hardly have done more to upset the plans of Lincoln, Stanton, and, perhaps most significantly, McClellan. Lincoln reacted precisely as Lee had predicted he would. He immediately ordered the military to take possession of "all the Railroads in the United States." Rather than sending McDowell and Shields to join McClellan as had been planned for the 26th, he directed McDowell to, "put twenty-thousand men in motion at once for the Shenandoah," to capture the forces of Jackson and Ewell. Shields's Division would return to the Valley as soon as they could get turned around from their recently completed eastward march to Manassas.

Frémont was at Franklin, 40 miles west of Harrisonburg, when he heard of the attack on Front Royal. Stanton somewhat ambiguously requested his assistance, "If you can operate so as to afford him [Banks] any support do so." Frémont responded with a litany of excuses. "Enemy seems everywhere re-enforced and active." "Beef is now secured, but during the last eight days there has been but one ration of bread, two of coffee and sugar, and nothing else." "Continued rains have flooded the streams." "I telegraph to General Meigs asking that he authorize the chief quartermaster and my quartermaster here to purchase immediately, wherever they may be had, 400 horses. Will you approve the requisition?" Lincoln had had enough and fired back that Frémont was "authorized to purchase the 400 horses or take them wherever or however you can get them. The exposed condition of General Banks makes his immediate relief a point of paramount importance." Frémont replied that, of course, he would do his best.

Brigadier-General Rufus Saxton won the Medal of Honor for "Distinguished gallantry and good conduct in the defense of Harper's Ferry, 26 to 30 May 1862," following Banks's retreat from Winchester. (LOC)

Lincoln's hope was to catch Jackson between three geographically separated but cooperating armies. Shields would travel through Manassas Gap to Front Royal and establish communications with Frémont, who would cross the Shenandoah Mountain to Harrisonburg. Banks would re-cross the Potomac and return to Winchester. Stanton had already sent Brig. Gen. Rufus Saxton to Harper's Ferry to command whatever troops could be rounded up there, and to assist Banks in any way he could. Saxton arrived on the morning of the 25th and immediately dispatched the 111th Pennsylvania Infantry toward Winchester, but recalled them when he learned of Banks's withdrawal from there.

After Jackson broke off his pursuit of Banks toward Martinsburg he debated the best course to follow next. On the 28th he sent Winder with four regiments toward Charlestown, in the direction of Harper's Ferry. They encountered Saxton's men and a short skirmish ensued, with the Union troops pulling back to the defenses Saxton had prepared on Bolivar Heights between the Potomac and Shenandoah Rivers west of Harper's Ferry. Winder advanced the next day with the intent of driving the Federal forces from the town, but when Jackson learned of Shields's approach on Front Royal and his pending confluence with Frémont, he began to recall his scattered troops to Winchester.

Shields arrived in Front Royal on the 30th, driving out the 12th Georgia Infantry assigned to guard it. In the process he recaptured a large amount of the supplies lost by Kenly the week before, and released several members of Kenly's 1st Maryland Infantry who had been kept there. Jackson was back in Strasburg by the 31st with the bulk of his command, less Winder's Brigade, and Shields was wondering where Frémont was.

Lincoln and Stanton were also wondering where Frémont was. On the 27th Lincoln received word that, instead of marching the 40 miles southeast from Franklin to Harrisonburg, Frémont had decided to march 40 miles northeast and was still west of Shenandoah Mountain. "I see that you are at Moorefield," Lincoln stated. "You were expressly ordered to march to Harrisonburg. What does this mean?" Frémont responded that he believed his task was to go to the relief of Banks, and to the best of his knowledge, Banks was in the vicinity of Winchester. "In executing any order received, I take it for granted that I am to exercise discretion concerning its literal execution, according to circumstances," he stated. His subsequent message added, "We are now moving with the utmost celerity possible in whatever direction the enemy may be found." Stanton wrote back telling Frémont to stay where he was "and wait orders."

While Lincoln and Stanton were engaged in an exchange of orders, counter-orders, and responses with Frémont, Jackson was pushing his men up the Valley. On June 1 Winder rejoined Jackson at Strasburg, having marched his men 36 miles in one day. "The command being again united, the retreat was resumed toward Harrisonburg," Jackson stated.

Cross Keys and Port Republic, June 8 and 9, 1862

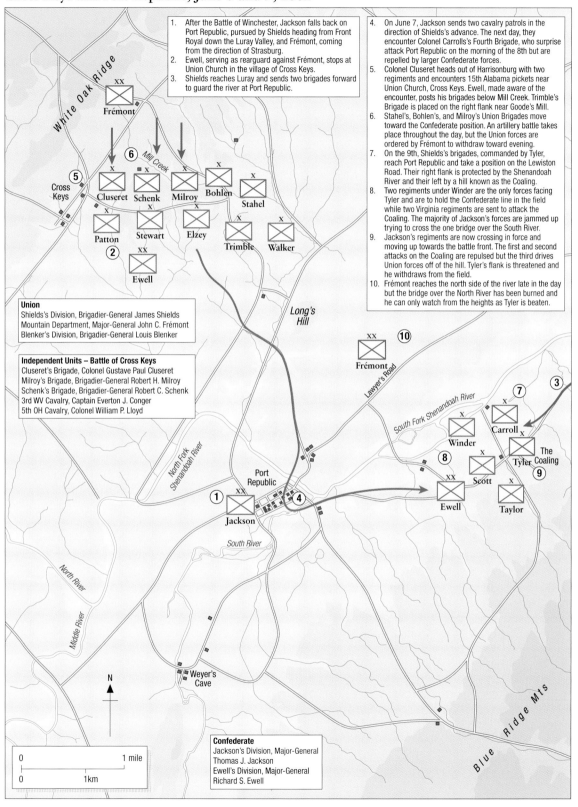

1. After the Battle of Winchester, Jackson falls back on Port Republic, pursued by Shields heading from Front Royal down the Luray Valley, and Frémont, coming from the direction of Strasburg.
2. Ewell, serving as rearguard against Frémont, stops at Union Church in the village of Cross Keys.
3. Shields reaches Luray and sends two brigades forward to guard the river at Port Republic.

4. On June 7, Jackson sends two cavalry patrols in the direction of Shields's advance. The next day, they encounter Colonel Carrolls's Fourth Brigade, who surprise attack Port Republic on the morning of the 8th but are repelled by larger Confederate forces.
5. Colonel Cluseret heads out of Harrisonburg with two regiments and encounters 15th Alabama pickets near Union Church, Cross Keys. Ewell, made aware of the encounter, posts his brigades below Mill Creek. Trimble's Brigade is placed on the right flank near Goode's Mill.
6. Stahel's, Bohlen's, and Milroy's Union Brigades move toward the Confederate position. An artillery battle takes place throughout the day, but the Union forces are ordered by Frémont to withdraw toward evening.
7. On the 9th, Shields's brigades, commanded by Tyler, reach Port Republic and take a position on the Lewiston Road. Their right flank is protected by the Shenandoah River and their left by a hill known as the Coaling.
8. Two regiments under Winder are the only forces facing Tyler and are to hold the Confederate line in the field while two Virginia regiments are sent to attack the Coaling. The majority of Jackson's forces are jammed up trying to cross the one bridge over the South River.
9. Jackson's regiments are now crossing in force and moving up towards the battle front. The first and second attacks on the Coaling are repulsed but the third drives Union forces off of the hill. Tyler's flank is threatened and he withdraws from the field.
10. Frémont reaches the north side of the river late in the day but the bridge over the North River has been burned and he can only watch from the heights as Tyler is beaten.

Union
Shields's Division, Brigadier-General James Shields
Mountain Department, Major-General John C. Frémont
Blenker's Division, Brigadier-General Louis Blenker

Independent Units – Battle of Cross Keys
Cluseret's Brigade, Colonel Gustave Paul Cluseret
Milroy's Brigade, Brigadier-General Robert H. Milroy
Schenk's Brigade, Brigadier-General Robert C. Schenk
3rd WV Cavalry, Captain Everton J. Conger
5th OH Cavalry, Colonel William P. Lloyd

Confederate
Jackson's Division, Major-General Thomas J. Jackson
Ewell's Division, Major-General Richard S. Ewell

"The pursuit of the enemy was continued to-day, and their rear again engaged. I hope to-morrow to force the rebels to a stand." Frémont to Stanton upon crossing the Shenandoah at Mount Jackson (pictured). (LOC)

In his operations from Front Royal to Charlestown, Jackson's troops had captured commissary supplies and Quartermaster stores valued at over $125,000, cavalry horses, and ordinance stores including "9,354 small-arms, and two pieces of artillery and their caissons." He reported 400 total casualties, consisting of 68 killed, 329 wounded, and three missing. Banks reported his total loss, including Kenly's command, as 62 killed, 243 wounded, and 1,714 captured, for a total of 2,019, along with 55 wagons "not, with but very few exceptions, abandoned to the enemy, but were burned upon the road."

Jackson arrived at Harrisonburg on the 5th, having been harassed the entire way from Strasburg by elements of Frémont's command, which had finally crossed Shenandoah Mountain on the evening of the 31st. Jackson was more concerned about the location of Shields's Division. "I became apprehensive that he was moving via Luray for the purpose of reaching New Market, on my line of retreat." Shields was indeed taking the Luray Road, hoping to fall on Jackson's flank while Frémont assailed him from the rear, but Jackson always seemed to stay one step ahead of him. Shields's advance reached the White House Bridge across the South Fork of the Shenandoah River, 4 miles southwest of Luray, on the afternoon of the 2nd. Jackson had already had it burned, along with the Columbia Bridge a few miles further south. With his route to New Market cut off, Shields proceeded south to the bridge at Conrad's Store near Swift Run Gap. Again, he was too late.

Jackson was moving fast and planning on the fly, anticipating the moves of the enemy as he went. If he could keep Frémont and Shields apart he could attack them separately. To everyone's surprise he fell back on Port Republic, a village located "in the angle formed by the junction of the North and South Rivers, tributaries of the South Fork of the Shenandoah." One bridge, connecting the town with the road to Harrisonburg, crossed the North River. Normally, the South River was fordable in places, but torrential rains had recently caused it to overflow its banks. Jackson encamped north of the town. Ewell was 4 miles up the road toward Harrisonburg, near Union Church, at the tiny village of Cross Keys.

Frémont reached Harrisonburg on the afternoon of the 6th. At about 4pm Ashby's cavalry surprised the 1st New Jersey Cavalry in woods on the southeast side of town, capturing their English commander Sir Percy Wyndham in the process. Believing that the Federals would make a more serious attack, Ashby called for infantry support. He mustered his forces in the woods on Chestnut Ridge hoping to ambush the Federal Infantry before they were ready to attack him. Lieutenant-Colonel Thomas L. Kane, leading the 13th Pennsylvania Reserve Battalion – the Pennsylvania Bucktails, did appear, though not from the direction Ashby expected. In the ensuing action Ashby's horse was shot from under him. Regaining his footing, he attempted to get his men to make a bayonet charge, but a bullet pierced his side and killed him. The Rebel infantry was now fully engaged and cleared the Federals from the field, capturing Colonel Kane in the process. With darkness falling both sides retired to their camps.

Jackson was greatly affected by Ashby's death. "The close relation which General Ashby bore to my command for most of the previous twelve months, will justify me in saying that as a partisan officer I never knew his superior; his daring was proverbial; his powers of endurance almost incredible; his tone of character heroic, and his sagacity almost intuitive in divining the purposes and movements of the enemy."

Despite Shields's inability to get across the Shenandoah River, he believed he had Jackson trapped. "The enemy had an impassable river in his front; Frémont's cannon were in his rear. This river could not become fordable in three days. It was only necessary to place him between Frémont's artillery and mine, with an impassable river in his front, to insure his destruction." As Shields advanced he became aware of rumors, although false, that General Johnston was sending Maj. Gen. James Longstreet with his 10,000-man division from Culpeper Courthouse through Thornton Gap to create a diversion for Jackson. He became concerned enough that he decided to stop at Luray with two of his brigades, while the other two advanced with orders to guard the river at Port Republic and cut the railroad at Waynesboro.

On the evening of the 7th Jackson sent two cavalry patrols across the South River in the direction of Shields's advance. Around 6pm the next morning they came "rushing back in disgraceful disorder announcing that the Federal forces were in close pursuit." Moments later, Shields's Fourth Brigade commander, Col. Samuel S. Carroll, came riding down the Luray Road with about 150 of the 1st West Virginia Cavalry and four artillery pieces. Seeing that the South River was fordable and the North River Bridge was still intact, with the town itself apparently protected only by a small force of cavalry, Carroll went on the offensive. He left two of his guns half a mile east of the bridge on Yost's Hill to fire on the enemy's cavalry. Once they ran off he crossed into the town, placed his other two cannons to guard the bridge and the street down which the cavalry had fled, and set about devising how best to hold the position until the rest of his brigade arrived.

No sooner had Carroll accomplished this feat than Taliaferro's Brigade, aroused by the sound of the guns, emerged from the woods near the bridge, strongly supported by 18 Rebel cannons. Colonel Fulkerson's 57th Virginia Infantry charged, sending the West Virginia cavalry fleeing in disarray and

The chance to end slavery brought Englishman Sir Percy Wyndham to America. McClellan assigned him to command the 1st New Jersey Cavalry because of his extensive experience in Austria and Italy. (LOC)

Note: Gridlines are shown at intervals of 1km (0.62 mile)

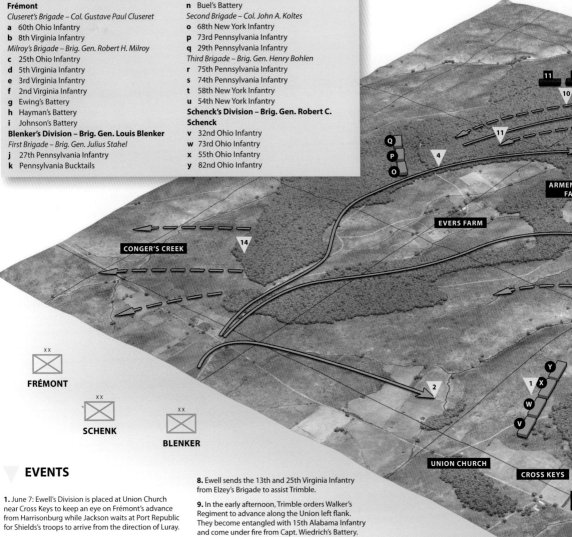

UNION FORCES
Frémont's Division – Maj. Gen. John C. Frémont
Cluseret's Brigade – Col. Gustave Paul Cluseret
a 60th Ohio Infantry
b 8th Virginia Infantry
Milroy's Brigade – Brig. Gen. Robert H. Milroy
c 25th Ohio Infantry
d 5th Virginia Infantry
e 3rd Virginia Infantry
f 2nd Virginia Infantry
g Ewing's Battery
h Hayman's Battery
i Johnson's Battery
Blenker's Division – Brig. Gen. Louis Blenker
First Brigade – Brig. Gen. Julius Stahel
j 27th Pennsylvania Infantry
k Pennsylvania Bucktails

l 8th New York Infantry
m 45th New York Infantry
n Buel's Battery
Second Brigade – Col. John A. Koltes
o 68th New York Infantry
p 73rd Pennsylvania Infantry
q 29th Pennsylvania Infantry
Third Brigade – Brig. Gen. Henry Bohlen
r 75th Pennsylvania Infantry
s 74th Pennsylvania Infantry
t 58th New York Infantry
u 54th New York Infantry
Schenck's Division – Brig. Gen. Robert C. Schenck
v 32nd Ohio Infantry
w 73rd Ohio Infantry
x 55th Ohio Infantry
y 82nd Ohio Infantry

▼ EVENTS

1. June 7: Ewell's Division is placed at Union Church near Cross Keys to keep an eye on Frémont's advance from Harrisonburg while Jackson waits at Port Republic for Shields's troops to arrive from the direction of Luray.

2. June 8, 8.30am: Cluseret's 8th West Virginia and 60th Ohio Infantry encounter pickets from the 15th Alabama Infantry posted near Union Church.

3. Reacting to the Union approach, Ewell places Steuart's Brigade on the left along the Mill Creek; Elzey is placed in the center; Trimble on the right.

4. Stahel's Brigade, following Cluseret, moves to the left in the direction of Trimble.

5. Milroy's Brigade and the Union artillery moved in to the left of Cluseret.

6. Trimble orders the 15th Alabama, 21st Georgia, and 16th Mississippi Infantry forward.

7. Around 11.00am, after his pickets are driven in by Stahel's lead elements, the 8th New York Infantry and the Pennsylvania Bucktail Rifles, Trimble orders a counterattack but pulls back when Bohlen's Third Brigade comes up in support of Stahel.

8. Ewell sends the 13th and 25th Virginia Infantry from Elzey's Brigade to assist Trimble.

9. In the early afternoon, Trimble orders Walker's Regiment to advance along the Union left flank. They become entangled with 15th Alabama Infantry and come under fire from Capt. Wiedrich's Battery.

10. Wiedrich's Battery has barely opened fire when it is inexplicably ordered to the rear under orders of the division commander, saving Walker's Regiment.

11. When Wiedrich's Battery is withdrawn Bohlen is forced to follow and fighting on this part of the battlefield comes to an end.

12. After an artillery duel lasting until mid-afternoon, Milroy, occupying the Union center, decides to move forward. The 25th Ohio Infantry leads the attack up a slope in tall grass that hides elements of Steuart's Brigade. Milroy attempts to flank the left side of the Confederate line, but is stopped by the 31st Virginia Infantry.

13. Milroy is then ordered back by Frémont.

14. By 6pm Frémont orders all Federal regiments to pull back to their morning starting positions. The battle is over.

THE BATTLE OF CROSS KEYS, JUNE 8, 1862

Frémont's Division attacks Ewell's Division, viewed from the west, 8am to 6pm

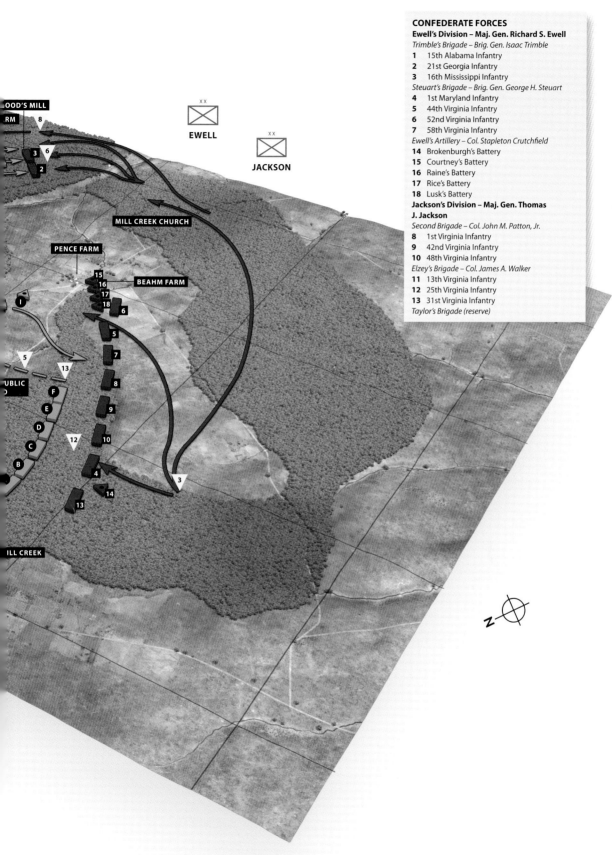

CONFEDERATE FORCES

Ewell's Division – Maj. Gen. Richard S. Ewell
Trimble's Brigade – Brig. Gen. Isaac Trimble
1   15th Alabama Infantry
2   21st Georgia Infantry
3   16th Mississippi Infantry
Steuart's Brigade – Brig. Gen. George H. Steuart
4   1st Maryland Infantry
5   44th Virginia Infantry
6   52nd Virginia Infantry
7   58th Virginia Infantry
Ewell's Artillery – Col. Stapleton Crutchfield
14 Brokenburgh's Battery
15 Courtney's Battery
16 Raine's Battery
17 Rice's Battery
18 Lusk's Battery

Jackson's Division – Maj. Gen. Thomas J. Jackson
Second Brigade – Col. John M. Patton, Jr.
8   1st Virginia Infantry
9   42nd Virginia Infantry
10 48th Virginia Infantry
Elzey's Brigade – Col. James A. Walker
11 13th Virginia Infantry
12 25th Virginia Infantry
13 31st Virginia Infantry
Taylor's Brigade (reserve)

OOD'S MILL
RM
EWELL
JACKSON
MILL CREEK CHURCH
PENCE FARM
BEAHM FARM
UBLIC
ILL CREEK

Z

"The attacks upon the enemy's rear of yesterday precipitated his retreat. General Ashby, who exhibited admirable skill and audacity, was among the killed." Frémont to Stanton, June 7, 1862. This sketch shows the 1st Maryland Cavalry attacking Ashby's troops. (LOC)

abandoning Carroll's guns. Carroll fell back, losing two of his guns in the process, as the Confederate artillery opened on his remaining two pieces on Yost's Hill. The rest of Carroll's infantry now came up, but "partially catching the contagion from the panic-stricken cavalry were retreating amid a heavy shower of shot and shell." Colonel Philip Daum, Shields's Chief of Artillery, arrived to direct the removal of the two guns from their exposed location. He quickly organized a more orderly withdrawal to a position about 2 miles north of the town, beyond range of the Rebel artillery. There Tyler's Brigade joined them. Taliaferro called off any further advance, but several miles to the west, near Cross Keys, Frémont had taken the field.

Colonel Gustave Cluseret led the 8th West Virginia and 60th Ohio Infantry out of Harrisonburg about the time Carroll was crossing the Port Republic Bridge. At around 8.30am they encountered the pickets of the 15th Alabama Infantry posted near the Union Church at the intersection of the Port Republic Road with the Keezletown Road, about a mile south of the main road to Harrisonburg. The skirmish alerted Ewell to the enemy's approach, providing him with ample time to post his brigades. His position was a strong one on slightly elevated ground, with woods on three sides and a large field in front. He placed Steuart on the left, within a mile of the Union Church. Elzey occupied the center with the artillery. Trimble was posted on the right.

Brigadier-General Julius Stahel's Brigade marched out of Harrisonburg behind Cluseret, continued another half mile along the Harrisonburg Road before turning off to the right and proceeding across the field in the direction of Trimble's Brigade. Milroy's column filed in on his right, along with the artillery. While awaiting the Federal advance, Trimble rode forward to examine a ridge that ran parallel to his line. Observing the natural strength of the advanced position, coupled with the cover provided by his artillery, he directed the 21st Georgia and 16th Mississippi Infantry to move forward. They were soon joined by the 15th Alabama Infantry, which had extricated itself from its position near the church.

Around 11am, the lead regiments of Stahel's Brigade, the 8th New York Infantry and the Pennsylvania Bucktail Rifles, began to drive in Trimble's

pickets. Trimble told his regiments on the ridge to hold their fire until the Federal troops were within about 50 paces of their position. This they did with deadly effect, forcing Stahel's men to fall back. Trimble then attempted a counterattack, partly in an attempt to capture one of the Federal batteries which had been brought up, but his regiments went in piecemeal and had to be called back to their starting position when Bohlen's Third Brigade was seen coming into line in response to a request for support from Stahel.

It was now after noon, and Ewell had sent the 13th and 25th Virginia Infantry under Col. Walker of Elzey's Fourth Brigade to Trimble's assistance. Trimble ordered Walker to lead his two regiments and the 15th Alabama Infantry "on my right through the woods and advance on the enemy in line perpendicularly to his line." Walker's regiments became entangled with the 15th Alabama Infantry and, in moving further to their right, exposed their flank to Bohlen's Brigade. The Virginians were caught behind a post fence, in clear line of the 74th and 75th Pennsylvania Infantry and Capt. Michael Wiedrich's Battery I, 1st New York Light Artillery. The Federal guns opened on the surprised Confederates but stopped after only a few rounds when they were directed to move to the rear, apparently by an order from the division commander Brig. Gen. Louis Blenker.

The withdrawal of Wiedrich's Battery saved Walker's regiments and exposed Bohlen's. As the guns withdrew, so did the 74th and 75th Pennsylvania Infantry. The 58th and 54th New York Infantry had no choice but to follow. By 3pm the 21st Georgia and 16th Mississippi Infantry had moved onto the ground previously occupied by Stahel's and Bohlen's brigades and the fighting on the eastern side of the battlefield came to an end.

The battle in the center had remained an artillery duel until mid-afternoon when Milroy, increasingly frustrated by the absence of any orders from Frémont, decided to go forward. With the 25th Ohio Infantry in the lead, his men came up a

Jackson had a temporary wagon bridge thrown across the South River at this spot, believed impassable by Shields, and crossed over his whole command for the attack on June 9, 1862. (Author's collection)

"Early on the morning of [June] the 9th, I told [Tyler] that if we could effect a retreat from our present position without disaster we would be doing as well as I could expect." Report of Col. Carroll of the engagement at Port Republic. (LOC)

slope in tall grass that hid the regiments of Steuart's Brigade. They were met by a galling fire from the Confederate 1st Maryland Infantry. Milroy attempted to slide to the right. If he had come up sooner he may have been able to flank Steuart's, and consequently Ewell's left, but the 31st Virginia Infantry arrived in time to stall the advance. Milroy still felt victory was in his grasp when a message from Frémont ordered him to pull back. Milroy was stunned, particularly when he saw Schenck's entire brigade unengaged to his right. By 6pm the Federal forces had withdrawn across the entire battlefield to their starting positions of the morning.

The Federal withdrawal was apparently prompted by a message Frémont received from Shields late in the afternoon. Shields outlined his plan to march towards Port Republic with his entire force on the 9th and catch Jackson between his army and Frémont's. Somehow believing that he had dealt Jackson a serious blow, Frémont elected to pull his

"I was ordered on the 7th by the general commanding to occupy the advance, and my division encamped for the night near Union Church." Report of Ewell on the battle of Cross Keys. (Author's collection)

men back from the battlefield at Cross Keys and wait for the morrow. Ewell was satisfied that he had done enough to keep Frémont off his tail and chose not to pursue the retreating Union troops, particularly after learning from Jackson that he intended to attack Shields the next day. The events of the 9th would decide the entire campaign.

After waiting all day on the 8th for Shields to follow up his advance with Carroll that morning, Jackson had decided that he would take the fight to Shields. As the day wore on, and Ewell was successfully beating back Frémont, Jackson formulated his plan. He directed Ewell to be prepared to follow him out of Port Republic at first light, leaving Trimble to burn the bridge that Carroll had fought to secure once the entire army was across the river.

Shields, with his two remaining brigades, was still at Luray, some 40 miles north of Port Republic, when he received word of Carroll's encounter that morning. He sent a message to Tyler directing that he and Carroll fall back on Conrad's Store, 15 miles north of Port Republic, where he would join them as rapidly as possible. He notified Frémont of his intent, and put his army in motion that evening, annoyed that Jackson had an escape route, but still believing that he had the advantage and would destroy Jackson's army the next day. He arrived at Conrad's Store at 9am on the 9th only to find that Carroll and Tyler had not pulled back as he expected, but were hotly engaged with Jackson and desperately in need of reinforcements.

After falling back the previous afternoon, Carroll and Tyler had surveyed the approach to Port Republic. Colonel Daum urged an attack with the combined force of infantry and artillery now available to them. Tyler, now observing the enemy's position for himself, stated that it appeared to him as "one to defy an army of 50,000 men," and "an attack upon it would result in the destruction of our little force." He received Shields's directive to withdraw to Conrad's Store and, believing he would have time in the morning to move out, ordered his men to bivouac for the night. At 4am he again rode forward with Carroll and learned from the pickets that there had been no movement from the enemy overnight. As he was having breakfast a little before 6am he received Shields's directive ordering them to "extricate themselves from their false position and fall back as speedily as possible." He was getting ready to reply when Jackson's artillery signaled that the engagement had begun.

Brigadier-General Winder, commanding the Stonewall Brigade, led Jackson's advance over a hastily constructed wagon bridge spanning the South River at 5am on the 9th. The crossing was severely hampered by the condition of the bridge and Winder's men filed slowly into line. To the north lay a 2-mile-long, 1-mile-wide swath of wheat and clover fields broken in places by wooden fences. On the left flowed the South Branch of the Shenandoah River. On the right, across the "turnpike" that ran north to Luray, and down which Shields's remaining two divisions were marching from Conrad's Store, were thick woods and dense underbrush rising up to the Blue Ridge. Bordering the north edge of the field was Lewiston Lane, which ran from the Lewiston Farm on the Luray Road west to the river. In the northeast corner, across the intersection of Lewiston Lane and the road, was the Lewiston Coaling – a steeply rising, 70ft-high mound built upon an old coal hearth.

Colonel Philip Daum recognized the dominating presence of the Coaling's position in relation to the fields below – the fields through which the Southern infantry would have to come if they were to attack the Union lines. There he emplaced six 10-pdr Parrott guns and a howitzer supported by the 66th Ohio Infantry. The Coaling had one vulnerability. According to Captain Joseph Clark, who commanded the Parrott guns, "Close to the flank was a ravine beyond which the ground rose rapidly giving a plunging fire upon our guns if occupied by the enemy."

Winder's lead unit, Colonel James W. Allen's 2nd Virginia Infantry, encountered Union pickets about a mile south of the main Federal line. Captain Joseph Carpenter's two guns drove them off and the advance continued. The firing of Carpenter's guns attracted the attention of Tyler as he was finishing his breakfast with his

"The army left Harrisonburg at 6 this morning, and at 8.30 my advance engaged the rebels about 7 miles from that place, near Union Church." Frémont to Stanton on the battle of Cross Keys. This sketch shows the march of Frémont's army through the woods in pursuit of Jackson. (LOC)

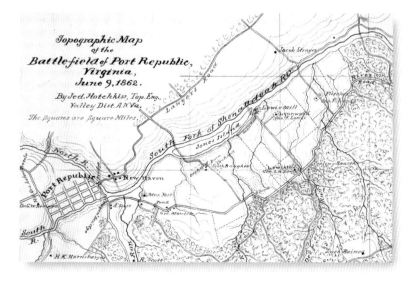

The "Topographic map of the Battle of Port Republic, June 9, 1862," from the Hotchkiss Collection. (LOC)

THE BATTLE OF PORT REPUBLIC, JUNE 9 (pp. 84–85)

On June 9, 1862, Stonewall Jackson attacked two brigades of Union Brigadier-General James Shields's Division under Brigadier-General Erastus B. Tyler, near the town of Port Republic. Brigadier-General Charles S. Winder, commanding the Stonewall Brigade, led Jackson's advance southeast through the town and across the South River at 5.00am. Turning north, the Rebels faced the prospect of crossing two miles of wheat and clover fields, crossed in places by wooden fences, to reach the Federal lines on Lewiston Lane. The Shenandoah River bordered the left and thick woods, across the Luray Road and rising up to the Blue Ridge, covered the right. To the northeast, across the intersection of Lewiston Lane and the Luray Road, was a steeply rising 70ft mound built upon an old coal hearth known as the Lewiston Coaling. The Union artillery commander, Colonel Philip Daum, recognized the dominating presence of the Coaling. He emplaced six 10-pdr Parrott guns and a howitzer there, supported by the 66th Ohio infantry, with a clear field of fire to the attacking Rebel infantry. Jackson understood the commanding position held by Tyler's artillery. He directed Winder to follow the small country lane that

ran from the river northeast through the fields to the Luray Road. Approaching the road, Colonel James W. Allen's 2nd Virginia Regiment encountered the Union pickets. Captain Joseph Carpenter brought up two of his guns, whose firing cleared the way for the infantry's continued advance towards the woods. Captain Joseph Clark, directing the Union Parrott guns on the Coaling, returned fire as Tyler began to deploy his regiments into line. Winder now ordered the 2nd and 4th Virginia, the latter under the command of Colonel Charles A. Ronald, with Carpenter's Battery, into the woods to the right of the road. Captain William T. Poague brought up his two Parrott guns **(1)** and Winder placed them in the wheat field left of the road to counter Clark's Parrotts and cover the infantry on the right. Colonel Andrew J. Grigsby's 27th Virginia **(2)** was ordered to support Poague's Battery, with Colonel J. H. S. Funk's 5th Virginia to his left. The Confederate artillery fire was completely ineffectual and the two regiments were forced to take a severe pounding **(3)** as they stood for nearly an hour waiting for the 2nd and 4th Virginia to reach and silence the Federal guns.

officers at the Lewiston House. Captain Clark returned fire as Tyler began to deploy his regiments across the Luray Road and along the lane. Daum saw Winder's men filing to his left and encouraged Tyler to sufficiently cover that direction, fearing a flank attack. The Confederate commander was preparing to do just that as he ordered the 2nd and 4th Virginia Infantry, the latter under the command of Colonel Charles A. Ronald, with Carpenter's Battery into the woods to the right of the road.

After twice being repulsed, Taylor pointed to the Coaling and shouted, "Men, you all know me. We must go back to that battery." (Author's collection)

More Confederate regiments were coming onto the field, and Winder began organizing his attack. Captain William T. Poague brought up his two Parrott guns and Winder placed them in the wheat field left of the road to counter Clark's Parrotts and cover the infantry on the right. Colonel Andrew J. Grigsby's 27th Virginia Infantry was ordered to support Poague's Battery, with Lt. Col. J. H. S. Funk's 5th Virginia Infantry to his left. For the next hour while the Rebels waited and hoped for the 2nd and 4th Virginian Infantry to reach the Federal guns, Poague tried to position his guns so as to have some impact on the Union artillery. The firing of Clark's Battery was so destructive that Winder was finally forced to send the 5th Virginia Infantry with one of Poague's guns to the left toward the river in an attempt to get around the Federal right flank.

Daum countered this move by sending two brass 10-pdr rifled guns from Captain James F. Huntington's Battery H, 1st Ohio Artillery, along with the remainder of Clark's Battery, to the Union right, 100ft shy of the river. Winder knew the only way he would be able to get his guns in a more favorable position to counter the Coaling battery fire, would be to drive off the Federal guns now on his left. Colonel Harry T. Hays had just reported with the 7th Louisiana Infantry and Winder placed him between the 5th and 27th Virginia Infantry and ordered them "to move forward, drive the enemy from his position, and carry his battery at the point of the bayonet."

Captain Clark was busy on the Coaling directing his battery's fire when Confederate riflemen "appeared in the woods covering the high ground and opened a sharp fire at a short range on our guns." These were the Virginians of the 2nd and 4th Virginia Infantry who had finally managed to work their way through the dense undergrowth, less the section of Carpenter's Battery that found it impossible to get through. Clark loaded his guns with canister and grapeshot, and, with the assistance of the skirmishers from the 66th Ohio Infantry, returned the fire of the enemy "with such destructive effect as to drive him immediately from his position." The two Virginia regiments fell back in disarray.

On the Confederate left Hays led his line across the wheat fields under the cover of his artillery. The Federal guns were returning fire but the Federal infantry was slow to get into position. The Rebels climbed over a fence and

Jackson's march to Mechanicsville, June 1862

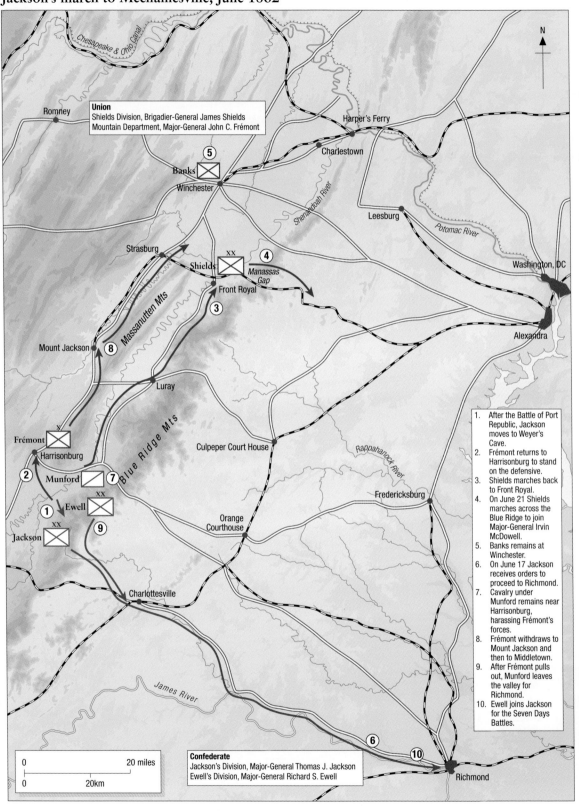

N

Union
Shields Division, Brigadier-General James Shields
Mountain Department, Major-General John C. Frémont

Romney

Harper's Ferry

Charlestown

Leesburg

Potomac River

5 Banks
Winchester

Strasburg

XX Shields

Manassas Gap

4

Front Royal

3

Washington, DC

Mount Jackson **8**

Massanutten Mts

Luray

Alexandra

Frémont **X**
Harrisonburg

Munford **7**

Blue Ridge Mts

Culpeper Court House

Rappahannock River

1 Ewell **XX**
9

Jackson **XX**

Orange Courthouse

Fredericksburg

Charlottesville

Shenandoah River

1. After the Battle of Port Republic, Jackson moves to Weyer's Cave.
2. Frémont returns to Harrisonburg to stand on the defensive.
3. Shields marches back to Front Royal.
4. On June 21 Shields marches across the Blue Ridge to join Major-General Irvin McDowell.
5. Banks remains at Winchester.
6. On June 17 Jackson receives orders to proceed to Richmond.
7. Cavalry under Munford remains near Harrisonburg, harassing Frémont's forces.
8. Frémont withdraws to Mount Jackson and then to Middletown.
9. After Frémont pulls out, Munford leaves the valley for Richmond.
10. Ewell joins Jackson for the Seven Days Battles.

James River

0		20 miles
0	20km	

Confederate
Jackson's Division, Major-General Thomas J. Jackson
Ewell's Division, Major-General Richard S. Ewell

6

10

Richmond

approached within 50 paces of the Federals when the 7th Indiana and 29th Ohio Infantry stepped into line on the south side of the Lewiston Lane and poured a devastating fire into them. The Rebels fell back behind the fence and tried to hold their ground, which they did for nearly an hour, but at a severe cost. Eventually, with no relief in sight and ammunition running low, they were forced to fall back and as they did the Federals advanced. The 5th and 7th Ohio Infantry, who

had lined up to the left of the 29th Ohio Infantry, managed to seize one of Poague's cannons. As Winder was attempting to rally his men around Col. John S. Hoffman's 31st Virginia Infantry, which had just come on to the field, action again shifted to the Coaling.

Jackson knew he had to silence the enemy's artillery and directed Brig. Gen. Richard Taylor to "take that battery." Taylor led his brigade, consisting of the 8th and 9th Louisiana Infantry and Wheat's Battalion, to the right into the same dense underbrush encountered by the 2nd and 4th Virginia Infantry, who were now attempting to reorganize following their repulse. The Louisianans stumbled blindly through the woods to the sound of the guns. Finally traversing the ravine and emerging on the slope of the Coaling, Taylor gave the order to charge. They were met by a volley from the 66th Ohio Infantry but pressed on and the 8th Louisiana Infantry reached the guns. The artillerymen put up as much resistance as was possible but were quickly overwhelmed. As soon as Tyler became aware of the fight on the hill he redirected some of the guns on the right of the field to fire toward the Coaling, and ordered the 5th and 7th Ohio Infantry to move from Winder's

Robert Parker Parrott was superintendent of the West Point Iron and Cannon Foundry when he invented the Parrott rifled gun in 1860. A rifled, muzzle-loading artillery piece, the 10-pdr was a significant improvement over the 12-pounder, smoothbore Napoleon. (Author's collection)

"The opposing forces fired in each other's faces," wrote Private George Neese, "bayonets gleamed in the morning sunshine." The Port Republic battlefield from the Coaling. (Author's collection)

front to support the 66th Ohio Infantry. Seeing the Federal counterattack the Louisianans began to kill the artillery horses to prevent the guns from being dragged from the field. The fighting developed into a riotous, bloody, hand-to-hand combat before the Rebels were again pushed back across the ravine.

It was now about 10am and across the river Frémont was just putting his men in motion. Schenck's Brigade, having barely participated in the action the day before, led

The Model 1841 12-pdr mountain howitzer could be broken down and transported by mule. Howitzers were effective anti-personnel weapons arcing canister over attacking infantry. (LOC)

the way, expecting to fight Ewell again on the same battlefield. They were disturbed to find that the only thing in front of them was the dead and dying from the previous day's action. Ewell was already gone.

By the time Frémont realized that the Rebels were gone, Ewell's brigades were across the bridge and racing down the Luray Road. They were approaching the woods at the same spot where Taylor had gone in with the idea of also striking the enemy's left flank, when they spotted what turned out to be the 5th and 7th Ohio Infantry turning to go to the fight on the Coaling. With his hat waving in the air as he ran, Ewell brought his brigades in on the flank of the Ohioans and poured in a staggering volley. The 5th and 7th Ohio Infantry were taken completely by surprise and fell back in disarray.

As Taylor's men were trying to regroup from their repulse on the hill, the surviving artillerymen, along with the 66th Ohio, and the 84th and 110th Pennsylvania Infantry who had come to their aid, were desperately trying to save the guns. They managed to haul one of the cannons away by hand, struggling through the mud on the top of the hill, but that was the best they could do. Taylor attacked again and the remnants of the 2nd and 4th Virginia Infantry joined in. To add to the spectacle, Ewell redirected his men from their attack on the Ohio regiments, and they too were bearing down on the Federal left.

The force of Taylor's attack was too much for the beleaguered Union troops on the hill. Winder had seen the Federal forces on his front being redirected towards the Coaling and he pressed his attack on the left with the 27th Virginia Infantry. Within minutes the entire Federal line was fleeing to the rear and Jackson ordered a general advance with every regiment under his command. As if to punctuate the futility of the past two days for the Union, Frémont now appeared on the bluffs across the river. He unlimbered his cannons and began to fire indiscriminately into the melee. It rapidly became apparent that he was much too late and was actually firing on the ambulances that had come onto the field to help the wounded.

Shields had advanced less than 10 miles from Conrad's Store when "a crowd of fugitives from the field gave evidence of retreat." He was attempting to bring some order to the chaos when the "main force came in sight, not, however, as fugitives or an army in retreat, but marching as proudly and calmly as if they were on parade." Close behind them came the Confederate cavalry, who turned about when they realized that fresh troops were to their front. Shields was in the process of notifying Frémont of his intent to continue his advance the next day when he received a note from McDowell. "It being the intention of the President that the troops of this department be employed elsewhere, the major-general commanding directs that you cease all further pursuit and bring back your division to Luray, and get ready for a march to Fredericksburg." A similar note went to Frémont. The campaign had come to an end.

AFTERMATH

After the battle Jackson camped at Weyer's Cave, just south of Port Republic, planning his next move. Frémont returned to Harrisonburg where he was directed to "Get your force well in hand and stand on the defensive," and to "await further orders, which will be sent to you." Shields marched slowly back to Front Royal and, on June 21, marched across the Blue Ridge to join Major-General Irvin McDowell. Banks remained in the vicinity of Winchester where he expected to send reinforcements to Frémont at the earliest opportunity. On June 12 he received a message from Frémont, stating that he had "beaten Jackson in two engagements and that Shields has been beaten on the opposite side of the river. Jackson has been re-enforced to the number of 30,000 or 35,000 men."

Jackson would have loved to have been reinforced to resume the Valley offensive, but on the 17th he received orders to proceed to Richmond. His cavalry, now under Col. Thomas T. Munford, remained in the vicinity of Harrisonburg harassing Frémont till he withdrew first to Mount Jackson and eventually Middletown. Once Frémont pulled out of Harrisonburg, Munford also marched to Richmond, where the forces of Jackson and Ewell joined with the main part of the Army of Northern Virginia during the series of battles known as the Seven Days.

The Valley Campaign made Stonewall Jackson an international celebrity. In a classic military campaign he used surprise and maneuver to win five significant victories with a force of about 17,000 against a combined force of over 50,000. William Wood, in his 1921 volume, *Captains of the Civil War*, sums it up:

> At McDowell, the Federals had 30,000 in strategic strength against 17,000 Confederates; yet the Confederates got 6000 on the field against no more than 2500. At Winchester, the Federal strategic strength was 60,000 against 16,000; yet the Confederate tactical strength was all of 16,000 against 7500 – one-eighth Banks's total. At Cross Keys, the strategic strengths were 23,000 Federals against 13,000 Confederates; yet 12,750 Federals were beaten by 8000 Confederates.

The typical Union soldier carried a musket, percussion cap box, cartridge box, bayonet and scabbard, canteen and knapsack, in addition to his personnel effects. This image shows an unknown Union volunteer. (LOC)

Confederate soldiers carried their possessions in a blanket roll worn across the shoulder and tied at the waist, along with a haversack, cartridge box, cap box, and musket. This image shows a Confederate soldier with an 1841 model Mississippi rifle. (LOC)

Finally, at Port Republic, the Federals, with a strategic strength of 22,000 against 12,700, could only bring a tactical strength of 4500 to bear on 6000 Confederates. The grand aggregate of these four remarkable actions is a Federal strategic strength of 135,000 against 58,700 Confederates. Yet in tactical strength the odds are reversed – 36,000 Confederates against 27,250 Federals. Stonewall Jackson, with strategic odds of nearly seven to three against him, managed to fight with tactical odds of four to three in his favor.

More importantly, he seriously disrupted McClellan's offensive, causing Lincoln to intervene personally to ensure that the Federal capital was safe from the threat of attack. Indeed, before the battles of Cross Keys and Port Republic were even fought, Lincoln had reconsidered the value of tying up his forces in the Valley, and had again stepped in to reorganize the army. McDowell's corps remained in the defense of Washington with only one division able to join McClellan on the Peninsula. After the campaign, the Army of Virginia was created under Maj. Gen. John Pope, incorporating the units of Banks, Frémont, and McDowell. Lee and Jackson soundly defeated this army in August at the second battle of Manassas/Bull Run, though without the participation of Frémont who refused to accept a position subordinate to Pope. He traveled to New York to await a subsequent assignment that never came.

Jackson's performance during the Peninsula Campaign was not his best but, once Lee rose to command of the Army of Northern Virginia on June 1, the combined forces of Jackson and Longstreet conducted a series of brilliant campaigns culminating in Jackson's most celebrated success at Chancellorsville in May 1863. It was also his last campaign. On May 3 while returning from a scouting party to locate the enemy's forward lines, Stonewall was accidentally shot by his own men and died a week later. An attempt to save his life by amputating his arm failed to stop the infection that spread through his body, causing Lee to say, "he has lost his left arm, but I have lost my right arm." Two months later, in a campaign that may have ended quite differently if Jackson had been there, Lee was soundly defeated at Gettysburg.

THE BATTLEFIELD TODAY

Most of the battlefield sites are accessible via driving tours only. The various organizations in the region have done exceptional service at providing information and access to the few sites that are open to the public. Both www.shenandoahatwar.org and www.civilwartrails.org are excellent sources on both the area and the battles.

First Kernstown – the Kernstown battlefield has two areas open to walking tours. The Pritchard-Grim Farm, site of Pritchard's Hill, is owned and managed by the Kernstown Battlefield Association, which maintains a number of interpretive markers and walking trails as well as an outstanding visitor orientation center. Visit www.kernstownbattle.org for more information. From Interstate 81, take Exit 310, Kernstown, Rt. 37W toward US 11. Take US 11 north for 2 miles to Battle Park Drive. Turn left to the entrance.

The Rose Hill Farm, site of the Stone Wall on Sandy Ridge, is owned and managed by the Museum of the Shenandoah Valley. The walking trail is open for self-guided tours on the third Saturday of each month April through October. Visit www.shenandoahmuseum.org for more information. From the Pritchard-Grim Farm, take US 11 north for 1.6 miles and turn left on Cedar Creek Grade. Follow Cedar Creek Grade for 1.9 miles and turn left onto Jones Road. Follow Jones Road for six-tenths of a mile.

McDowell – A Virginia Civil War Trails pull-off and sign on highway US 250, marks the trailhead of a rigorous 45-minute hike to the top of Sitlington's Hill. To reach the battlefield from Staunton, VA, follow US 250 west for approximately 26 miles.

Front Royal – Printed driving and walking tours of the ten key battle sites are available from the Front Royal Visitor Center, 414 East Main Street, which is worth a stop in itself.

Winchester – A printed battlefield driving tour guide, entitled *Winchester at War*, which encompasses nine stops covering both Kernstown and Winchester, is available at most Civil War sites. Visit www.shenandoahatwar. org for more information.

Cross Keys and Port Republic – A printed battlefield driving tour guide for both battles is available at most Civil War sites and at the Hardesty-Higgins House Visitor Center in Harrisonburg, www.harrisonburgtourism. com. Start at the Civil War Orientation Center, located inside the Visitors Center, 212 South Main Street at the Hardesty-Higgins House in Harrisonburg, VA.

FURTHER READING

By far, the most important source of first-hand information on not only Jackson's Valley Campaign, but also the American Civil War as a whole, can be found in the 128-volume *War of the Rebellion, Official Records of the Union and Confederate Armies*. Many of the well-known books on the campaign, particularly Henderson and Vandiver, focus on the "genius" of the "Mighty Stonewall," telling the story primarily from the Southern point of view. More recently, perhaps due to the Sesquicentennial of the Civil War, there has been a resurgence of interest in this topic and authors like Ecelbarger and Cozzens offer a more even-handed analysis of the events.

Cozzens, Peter, *Shenandoah 1862: Stonewall Jackson's Valley Campaign*, Chapel Hill, NC: University of North Carolina Press, 2008

Ecelbarger, Gary L. *"We are in for it!": The First Battle of Kernstown*, Shippensburg, PA: White Mane Publishing Company, Inc. 1997

Faust. Patricia L., (ed.) *Historical Times Illustrated Encyclopedia of the Civil War*, New York: Harper & Row, 1986

Freeman, Douglas Southall, *Lee's Lieutenants, Vol. I, Norwalk*, CT: Easton Press Edition, 1991

Harper's Pictorial History of the Civil War, New York: The Fairfax Press, 1987

Henderson, G. F. R., *Stonewall Jackson and the American Civil War, Vol. I*, London: Longmans Green & Co., 1913

Hotchkiss, Jedediah, *Make Me a Map of the Valley, The Civil War Journal of Stonewall Jackson's Topographer*, Dallas, TX: Southern Methodist University Press, 1973

Johnston, Joseph E, *Narrative of Military Operations, Directed During the Late War Between the States*, New York: D. Appleton and Company, 1874

Sears, Stephen W., (ed.) *The Civil War Papers of George B. McClellan*, Boston, MA: Da Capo Press, 1992

Vandiver, Frank E., *Mighty Stonewall*, Norwalk, CT: Easton Press Edition, 1996

War of the Rebellion, *Official Records of the Union and Confederate Armies, Series I, Vol. 2, Vol. 5, and Vol. 12*, Harrisburg, PA: The National Historical Society, 1971

Wood, William, *Captains of the Civil War, A Chronicle of the Blue and the Gray*, New Haven, CT: Yale University Press, 1921

INDEX